BUILDINGS, BRIDGES AND Landmarks

A COMPLETE HISTORY

P9-CNF-509

CONTENTS

ThunderBay
P·R·E·S·S

Thunder Bay Press
An imprint of Printers Row Publishing Group
10350 Barnes Canyon Road, Suite 100, San Diego, CA 92121
www.thunderbaybooks.com

Copyright © Quarto Children's Books Ltd, 2016

All rights reserved. No part of this publication may be reproduced, distributed, or transmitted in any form or by any means, including photocopying, recording, or other electronic or mechanical methods, without the prior written permission of the publisher, except in the case of brief quotations embodied in critical reviews and certain other noncommercial uses permitted by copyright law.

Printers Row Publishing Group is a division of Readerlink Distribution Services, LLC. The Thunder Bay Press name and logo are trademarks of Readerlink Distribution Services, LLC.

All notations of errors or omissions should be addressed to Thunder Bay Press, Editorial Department, at the above address. All other correspondence (author inquiries, permissions) concerning the content of this book should be addressed to Quarto Children's Books Ltd, 6 Blundell Street, London N7 9BH, UK.

ISBN: 978-1-62686-556-3

Manufactured in Shenzhen, China
20 19 18 17 16 1 2 3 4 5
Paper engineer Bag of Badgers; **Designer** David Ball; **Illustrators** Stefano Azzalin, Jani Orban;
Editor Suhel Ahmed; **Managing Editor** Diane Pengelly; **Creative Director** Jonathan Gilbert; **Publisher** Zeta Jones

HOW TO BUILD YOUR MODELS

BASIC TECHNIQUES

Assemble the landmark models following the instructions and photographs detailed for each model from page 103 onward. The basic techniques you'll be using to build most of the models are illustrated here.

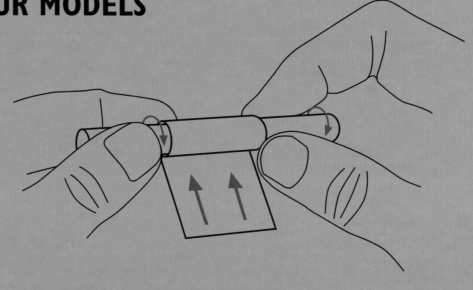

ROUNDING: Where rounded pieces are required, use a round pencil to help shape the piece of card. Wind the piece carefully around the pencil, keeping the tension even as you turn, and then release.

SHAPING: Before assembling the model, roll the columns into curved shapes along the creased lines, using the photograph of the finished model as a guide.

INTRODUCTION

A landmark usually refers to a natural feature like a mountain or a promontory—something you can see on a map. But we have been building our own landmarks since the pharaohs commissioned the Pyramids or the Druids built Stonehenge, and doubtless long before that. Landmarks do more than help us find our way around the world; they demonstrate progress and the triumph of the human race over the natural elements of storms, freezing temperatures, and scorching sun. They give us shelter but they also represent our dreams.

Each of the 25 buildings covered by the main part of the book is put into its historical and geographical context. Features include the date of the building's construction, its height and size, the names of the person who commissioned the building and the architects, the materials used, as well as the purpose and the cost

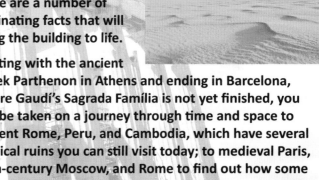

(where known). The main architectural elements are described and there are a number of fascinating facts that will bring the building to life.

Starting with the ancient Greek Parthenon in Athens and ending in Barcelona, where Gaudí's Sagrada Família is not yet finished, you will be taken on a journey through time and space to ancient Rome, Peru, and Cambodia, which have several magical ruins you can still visit today; to medieval Paris, 16th-century Moscow, and Rome to find out how some of Europe's finest cathedrals were built; to castles and fortifications in Japan, China, and Germany; to temples in India and mosques in Africa; to government buildings

CREATING THE DOMES:
When building the domed pieces, fold down the strips so that the edges are touching, and then wrap the bottom strip around the base to secure the dome structure.

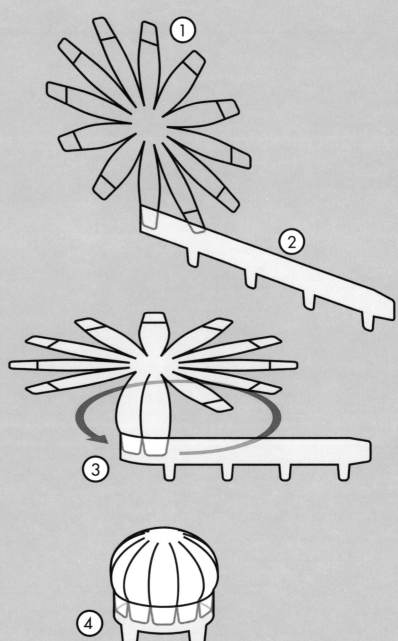
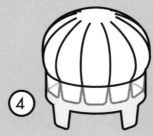

in Washington, D.C., and London. You will see how the great engineers of the 19th and 20th centuries built monuments and bridges in the United States, Australia, the UK, and Brazil. And you will also travel to New York City and Toronto to see how some of the world's highest towers were built. It will be a fascinating journey.

The final part of the book covers 20th- and 21st-century buildings. These "Eleven Modern Wonders of the World" were designed by some of the best architects, most of whom are still working today. These include buildings from all over the world and show that builders and designers have lost none of the ingenuity of their predecessors. In addition, they now have the help of computers and modern techniques so they can realize architectural visions in ways that used to be impossible.

The landmark buildings illustrated and written about in this book were constructed over a period of 2,500 years. Now you can punch out the cardboard pieces and build your own Parthenon, your own Eiffel Tower, and your own Empire State Building. You will be following in the footsteps of the architects and builders—some famous, some unknown—who have made the world look the way it does today. And you can put together all the world's best buildings in one place—your home.

SLOTTING: To secure card pieces together, push the tabs into the slots, making sure you match them up correctly so that the numbers correspond; i.e., tab 1 goes into slot 1, tab 2 into slot 2, and so on.

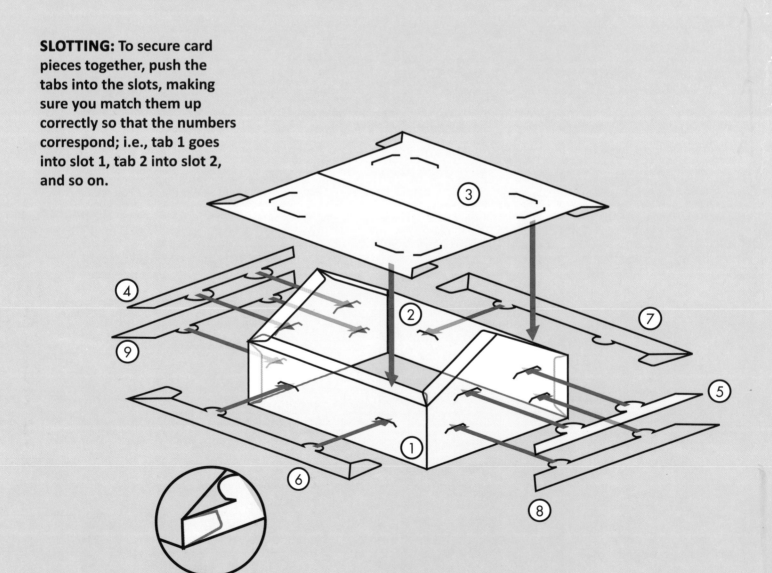

ANGKOR WAT

Angkor Wat in Cambodia is the largest religious building in the world. Built in the early 12th century by the Khmer king Suryavarman II, it was originally a Hindu temple, which was later converted into a Buddhist temple and mausoleum for its founder. Modern excavation of the site, led by a French team, began in 1908; its restoration was suspended during the Khmer Rouge era in the 1970s.

The irrigation system was based on reservoirs, which allowed the cities to survive and prosper for many centuries. **15**

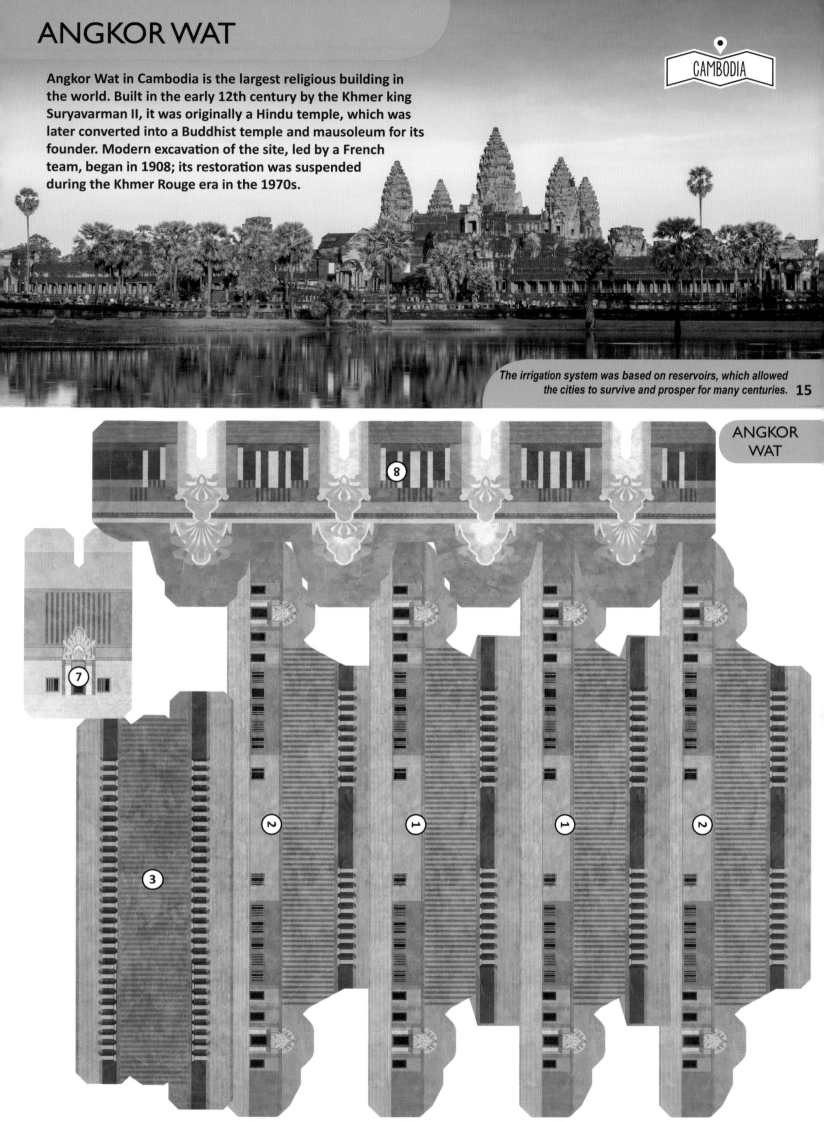

ANGKOR WAT

FEATURES:

- *Date of construction* 12th century
- *Height* 158 feet
- *Size* 495 acres (whole site)
- *Commissioner* King Suryavarman II
- *Architect* Unknown
- *Material* Brick
- *Purpose* Temple, palace, and mausoleum

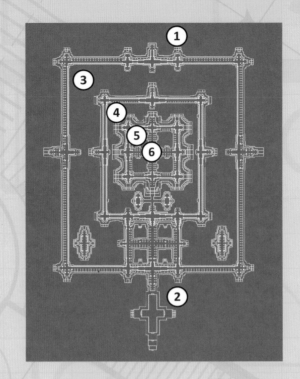

The total site covers an area of 495 acres and measures 4,920 feet by 4,265 feet. The area enclosed by the stone wall is 198 acres and measures 3,360 feet by 2,625 feet. The moat is 620 feet wide. Access to the temple is by an earth bank to the east (1) and a sandstone causeway to the west (2).

The temple stands on a terrace that dominates the city. It is made of three rectangular galleries (3, 4, 5) rising to a central tower (6), each level higher than the last, giving the site its characteristic profile.

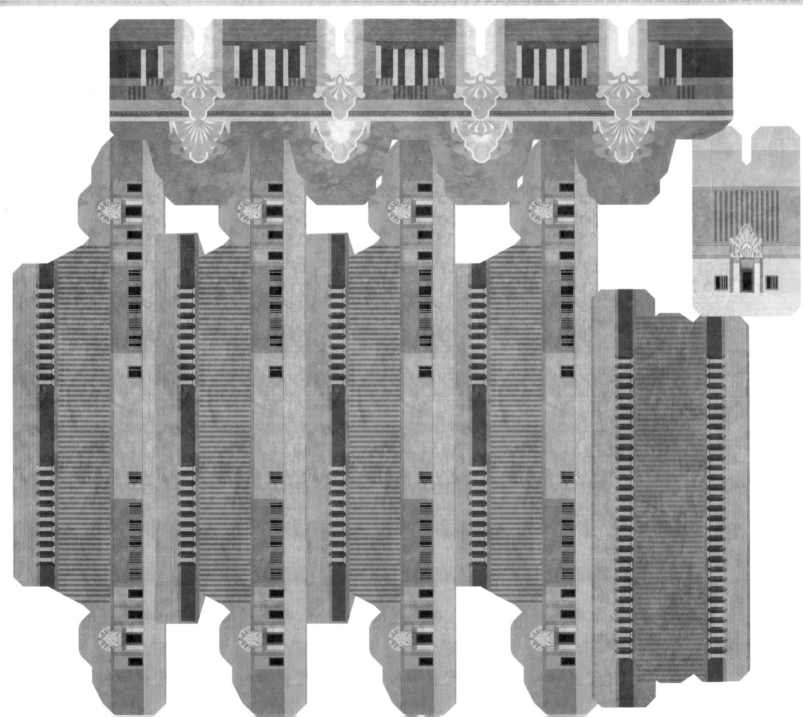

ARCHITECTURAL ELEMENTS

The Khmer Empire ruled much of Southeast Asia and played a significant role in the cultural development of the region. Angkor Wat represents all that remains of that civilization. Khmer architecture evolved from Indian architecture, but it developed its own character and adopted many of the characteristics of other cultures. Angkor Wat therefore has architectural as well as religious and symbolic significance.

▲ The exposed roots of a Ficus strangulosa *tree frame the entrance to the ancient ruins.*

▶ *The carved faces of the statues in the Ta Prohm temple area.*

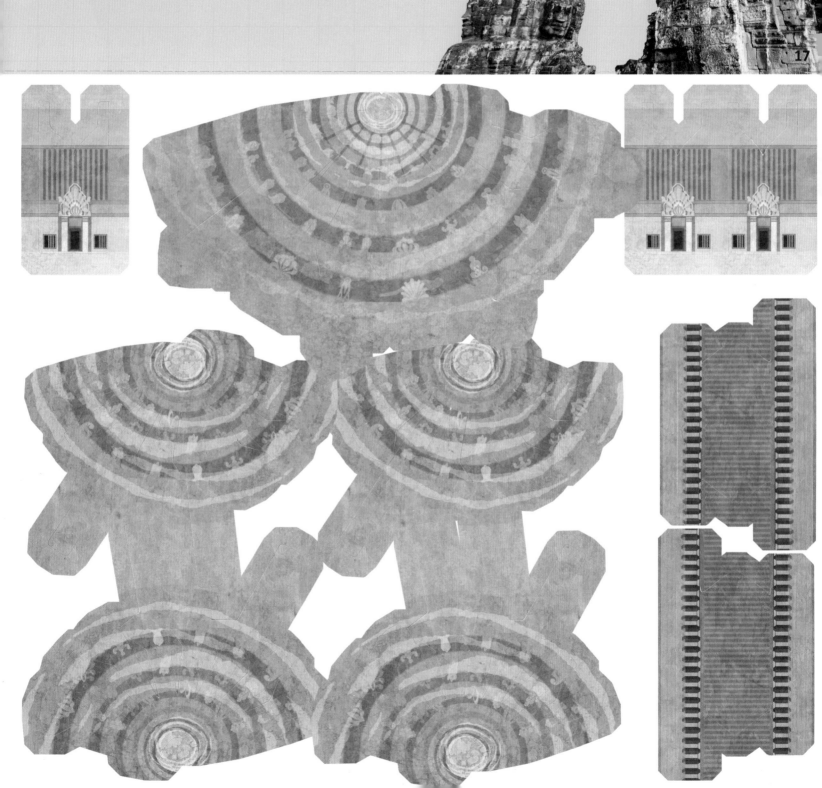

▼ *The entrance to the tower structures of Angkor Wat.*

FASCINATING FACTS

• According to legend, the temple was constructed in a single night by the god Indra. The fact that the stone had to be transported from a quarry more than 20 miles away suggests it took several decades.

• Angkor Wat's preservation is largely due to the fact that its moat prevented the jungle from encroaching and destroying the stonework.

▶ *Reflections of the Bayon temple Angkor Thom, with canoes in the foreground.*

NOTRE-DAME DE PARIS

Notre-Dame stands in splendid isolation on Île de la Cité, but three attempts were needed to clear the houses nearby: in the 12th century, in the 19th century (part of Baron Haussmann's renovation of Paris), and again in the 1960s.

Parisians call the cathedral "the Forest." In most churches the structure is stone, but here they used wood to build the original structure in the 12th century. Now only the cathedral's choir is made of the original wood.

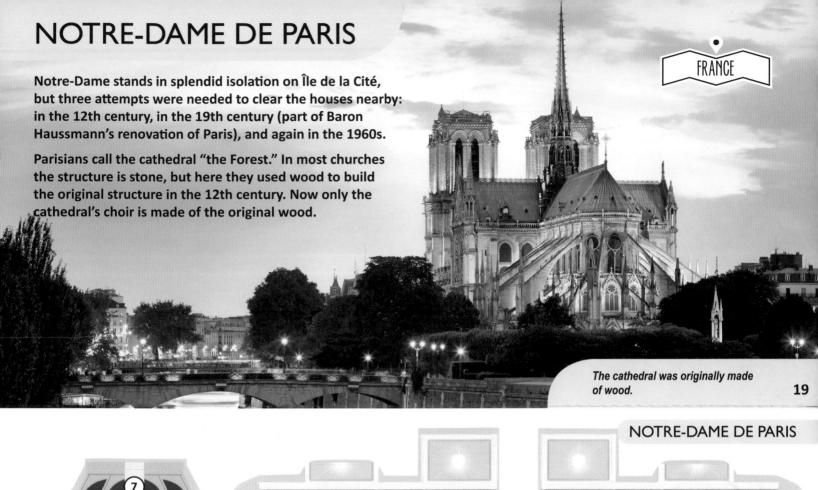

The cathedral was originally made of wood.

19

NOTRE-DAME DE PARIS

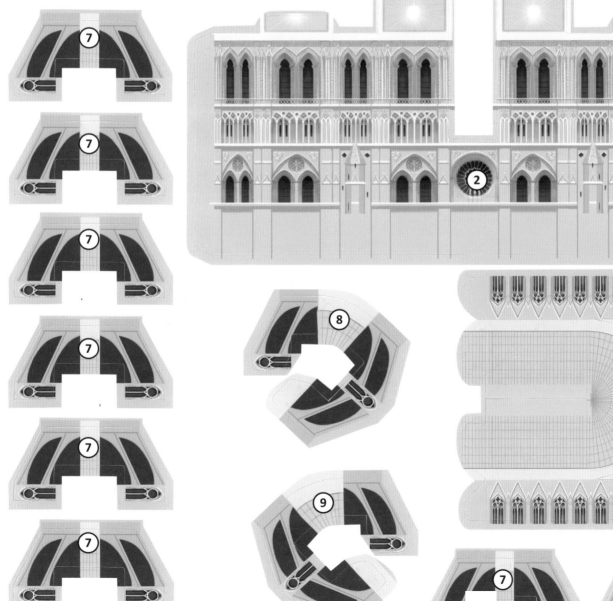

FEATURES:

- *Date of construction* 1163–1345
- *Height* 197 feet (nave), 315 feet (spire)
- *Size* 420 x 131 feet (transept)
- *Commissioner* Maurice de Sully, Bishop of Paris
- *Architects* Jean de Chelles, Pierre de Montreuil, Pierre de Chelles, Jean Ravy, Jean le Bouteiller
- *Materials* Limestone and wood
- *Purpose* Place of Christian worship

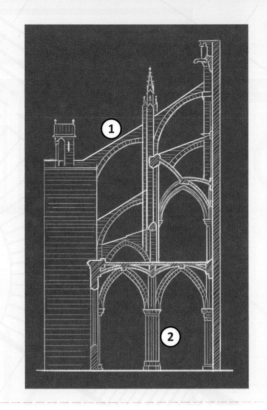

Notre-Dame was one of the first buildings to use flying buttresses (1)—arched supports that carry the weight of the roof via stone columns (2), preventing the walls from being pushed out by the weight above them. The use of flying buttresses freed up medieval architects, enabling them to replace much of the stonework of their cathedrals with glass, filling them with light.

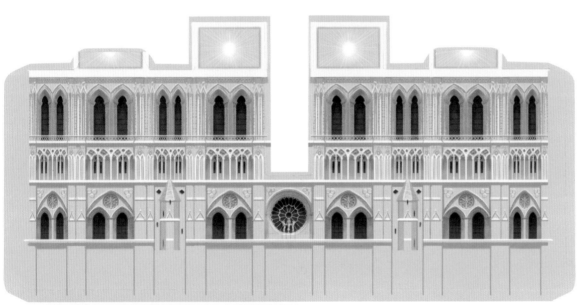

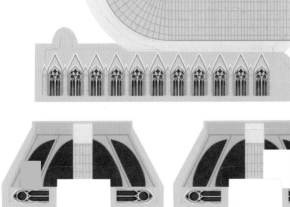

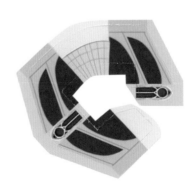

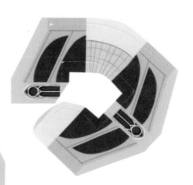

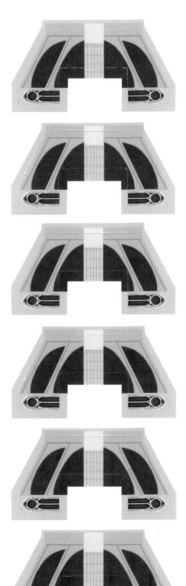

◄ *The Emmanuel Bell in the south tower of Notre-Dame, showing the wooden structure of the roof.*

▼ *A pair of gargoyles on the roof of Notre-Dame appear to be in conversation.*

ARCHITECTURAL ELEMENTS

Prompted by writer Victor Hugo and artist Ingres, who draw attention to Gothic styling, 19th-century architect Eugène Emmanuel Viollet-le-Duc restored the sculptures on the west facade, where three magnificent portals had been damaged in the revolution. He added and replaced windows and, as was common among his Victorian counterparts in England, added new features: the spire and the sacristy. The spire replaced a bell tower from 1250, which was taken down between 1786 and 1792.

▶ *The 19th-century spire of Notre-Dame replaced the original bell tower.*

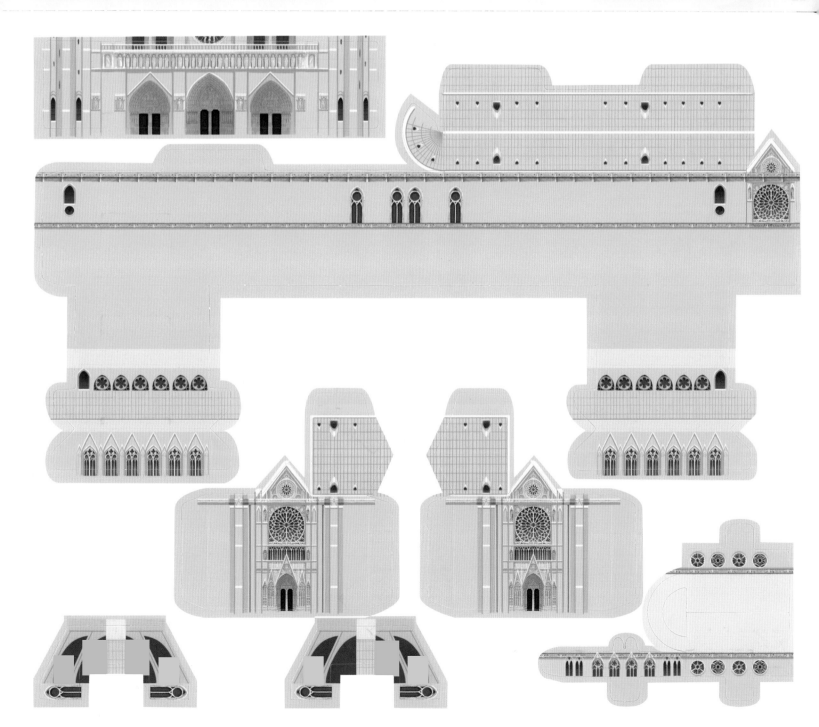

FASCINATING FACTS

• Notre-Dame is effectively the center of Paris as, since 1768, all distances in France have been measured from Notre-Dame.

• A fire during the 1871 Paris Commune was started when Communards piled chairs in the nave and set light to them. The church escaped largely undamaged.

• During the revolution, the cathedral was used as a warehouse for the storage of food.

◀ *An 1850 illustration of the new sacristy published in the Magasin Pittoresque.*

▶ *A contemporary view of the nave, which is 226 feet wide.*

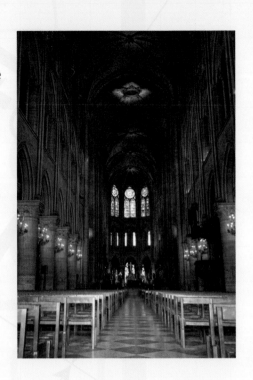

22

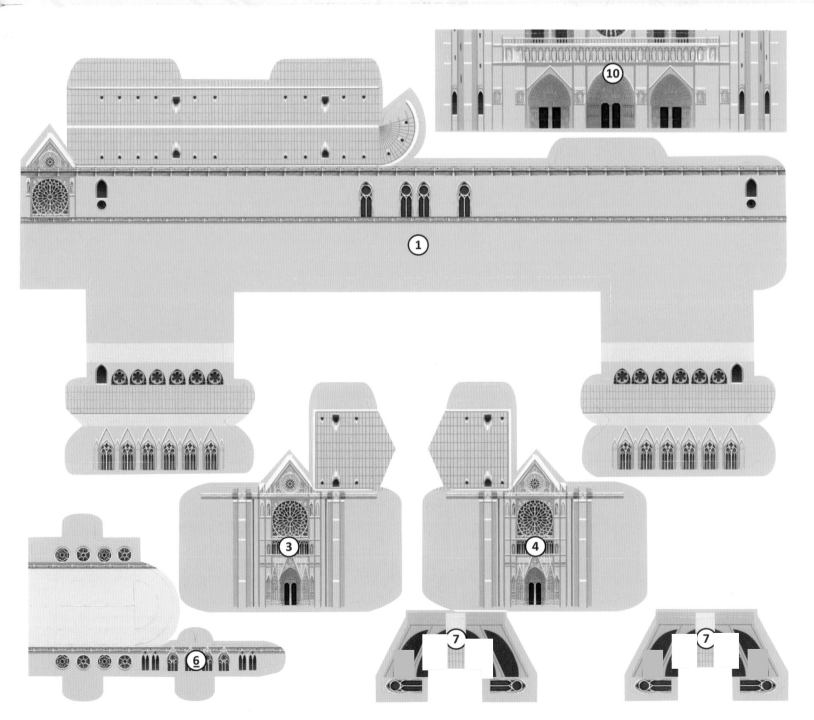

ST. BASIL'S CATHEDRAL

The original building, Trinity Cathedral, was built in Moscow between 1555 and 1561 to commemorate Ivan the Terrible's victories in the Russian campaigns against Kazan and Astrakhan. Eight small churches were built encircling a ninth, the Cathedral of the Intercession, all sharing foundations and a crypt and joined by two galleries. A tenth church was added to the complex in 1588 above the final resting place of the venerated local Saint Vasily (Basil).

The main part of the cathedral is really nine buildings in one.

23

ST. BASIL'S CATHEDRAL

FEATURES:

- *Date of construction* 1555–1561
- *Height* 187 feet (Cathedral of the Intercession)
- *Size* 689 square feet (internal area of the Cathedral of the Intercession)
- *Commissioner* Ivan the Terrible
- *Architect* Postnik Yakovlev
- *Materials* Brick, stone, wood frame, stucco, ceramics, and gilded tin
- *Purpose* Place of Christian worship

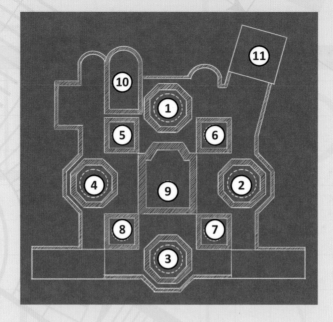

The plan of nine of the churches is perfectly symmetrical, with four octagonal churches (1, 2, 3, 4) alternating with four additional churches (5, 6, 7, 8) arranged around the central church (9). However, the symmetry is broken by the tombstone-shaped Church of St. Vasily (10), and by the bell tower to the southeast (11).

We know that the central church, the Cathedral of the Intercession, was the last to be completed. The church building record includes the precise date—June 29, 1561.

ARCHITECTURAL ELEMENTS

The profile of the cathedral resembles a vast bonfire, whose flames twist into the sky. Its style is appropriately Byzantine, yet it is unlike any other Russian building of the previous millennium, or any other Byzantine building. It is a somewhat bizarre mixture of stylistic influences, including Russian traditions of wooden and stone building, with elements of Italian and Greek architecture. The brickwork in the vaults is distinctly Italianate.

◄ *Looking up to the painted ceiling of St. Basil's Cathedral.*

▶ *The brightly colored onion domes of the Cathedral of Vasily the Blessed.*

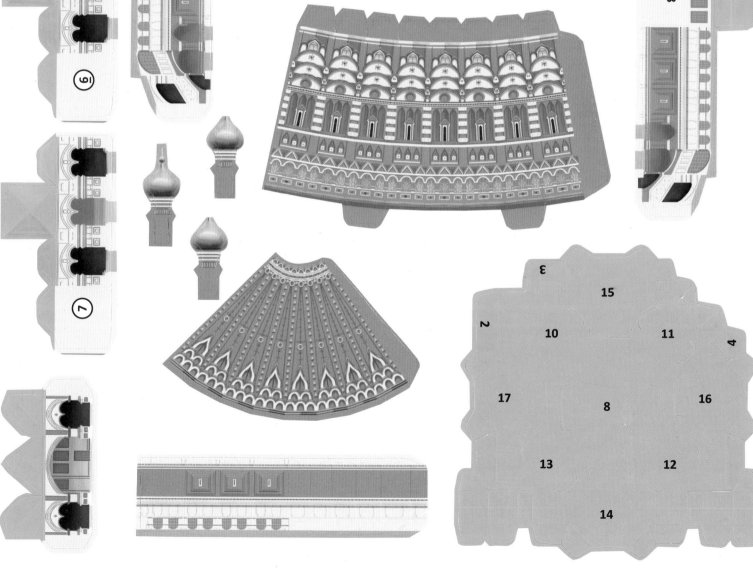

FASCINATING FACTS

• The cathedral was secularized in the late 1920s by Joseph Stalin, and has since been part of the State Historical Museum—and of the Kremlin complex.

• According to legend, Ivan the Terrible had the architect blinded after the completion of his masterpiece, so that he could not reuse the plans elsewhere—a move prospective clients must have taken seriously. However, in reality the sighted Postnik Yakovlev continued to practice as an architect throughout the 1560s.

◄ *A portrait of Ivan the Terrible, tsar of Russia from 1547 to 1584.*

▶ *Russian one-ruble stamp showing St. Basil's Cathedral.*

▲ *An engraving from 1875 of St. Basil's Cathedral, published in the* Industrial Encyclopedia.

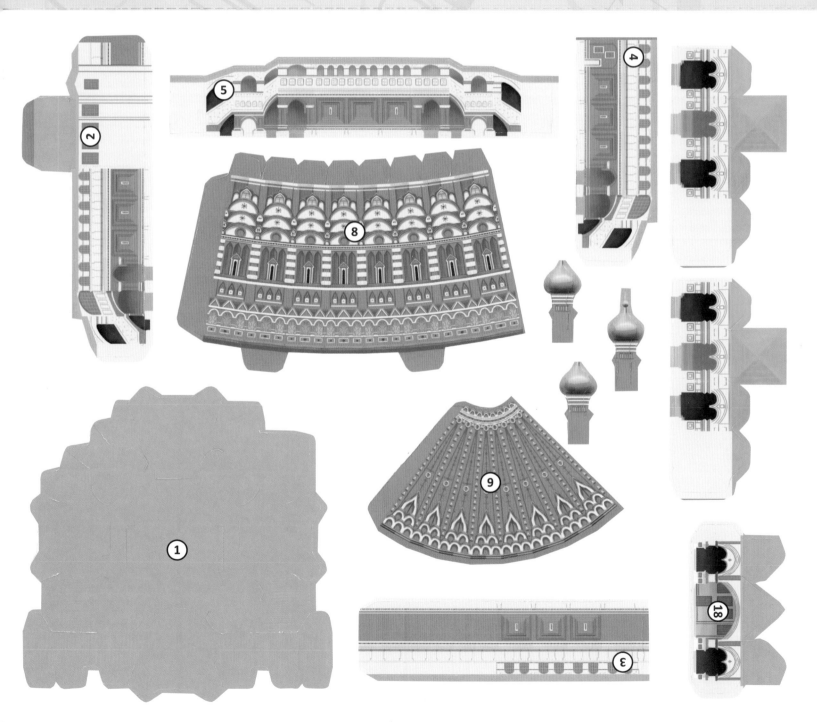

HIMEJI-JO

This castle is popularly known by its nickname of Shirasagi-jo—or White Heron Castle—because its central building resembles a bird taking flight. Most of what we see today dates from the early 17th century. The centerpiece is the Tenshu-gun, which comprises the six-story fortress, with three smaller fortresses and a series of ramparts.

The castle is named for its resemblance to a bird spreading its wings.

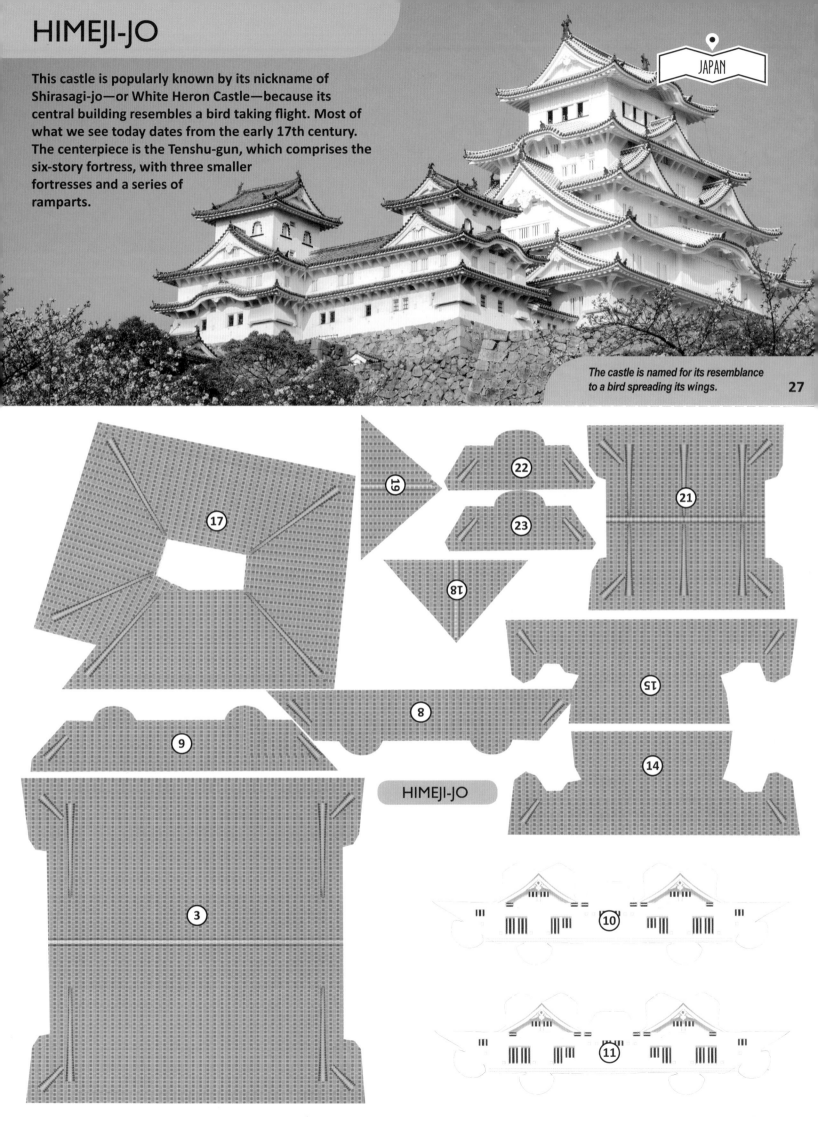

HIMEJI-JO

FEATURES:

- *Date of construction* 1333–1618
- *Height* 152 feet (main tower)
- *Size* 576 acres, including the 83 buildings and surrounding land within the walls
- *Commissioners* Akamatsu Norimura (1333–1346), Ikeda Terumasa (1601–1609)
- *Architects* Akamatsu Norimura (1333–1346), Toyotomi Hideyoshi (1581), Ikeda Terumasa (1601–1609), Honda Tadamasa (1617–1618)
- *Materials* Wood, stone, earth, plaster, and tile
- *Purpose* Defense and residence

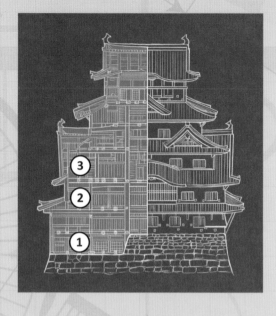

Elevation drawing of Himeji-jo's main donjon (fortified tower), a seven-story wooden building dating from 1609. The drawing was part of a major rebuilding of the original castle undertaken by daimyo (feudal baron) Ikeda Terumasa.

The room occupying the first story (1) is known as the "Thousand Mat Room," after the straw tatami mats that cover the floor. The third (2) and fourth (3) stories feature stone-throwing platforms from which soldiers could defend the castle.

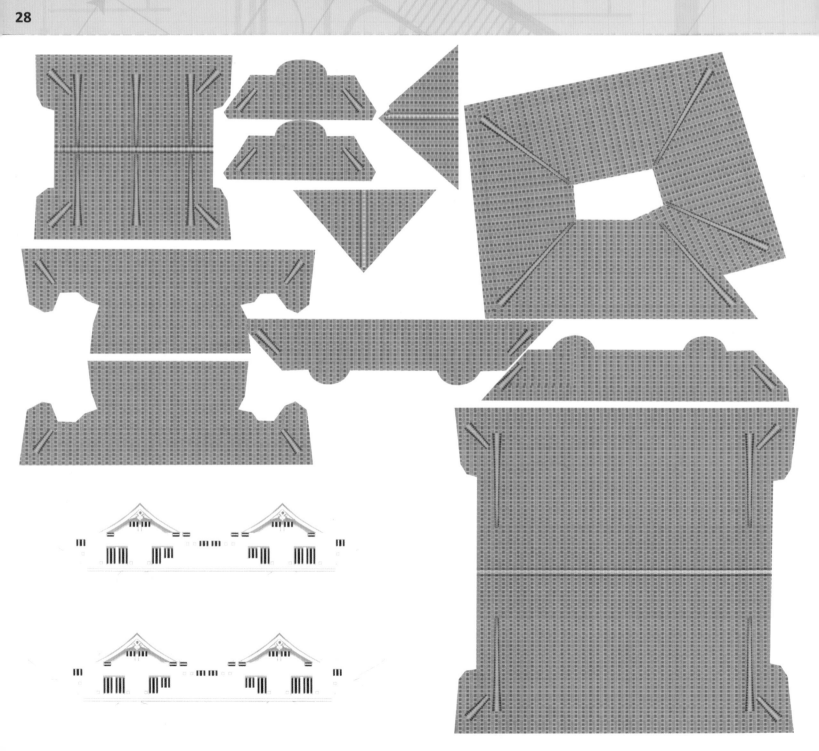

ARCHITECTURAL ELEMENTS

Himeji-jo represents the epitome of Japanese castle architecture in wood, and with all its significant features still intact. The main tower's structure is provided by just two 87-foot poles, tapering from 3.1 feet at their base and roughly hewn, according to the concept of *wabi-sabi*—the beauty of imperfection.

▶ *The multilayered roof, visible throughout the city of Himeji.*

▲ *One of the corridors inside the castle— almost all the internal fittings are original.*

▲ *Detail of the delicate carvings on Himeji-jo.*

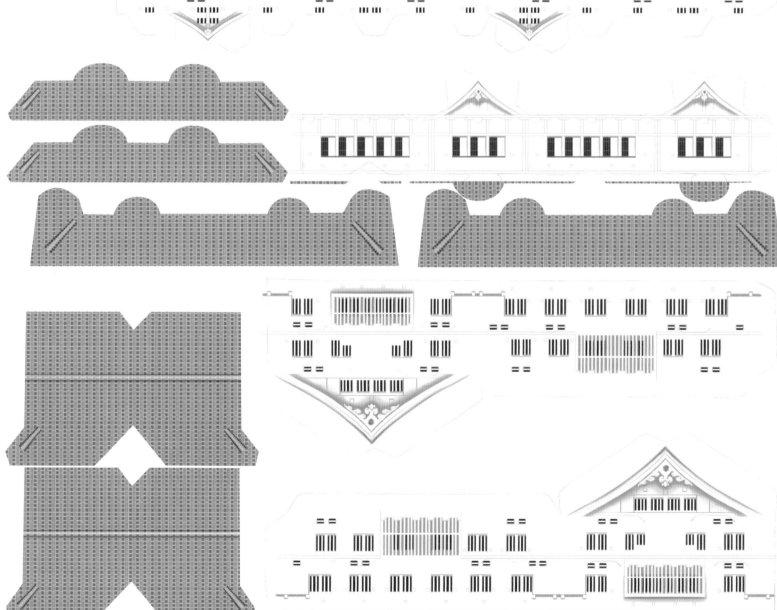

FASCINATING FACTS

• The castle functioned as the center of a feudal domain for more than five centuries until 1868, when Tokugawa Yoshinobu resigned as shogun and surrendered his powers to Emperor Meiji.

• The castle has survived because it has been untouched by war. In fact, the only recorded battle to have taken place within its walls was during the filming of the James Bond film *You Only Live Twice*.

◀ *A collection of ancient Japanese crests on display in the castle.*

▲ *In the springtime, cherry blossom trees frame the main tower.*

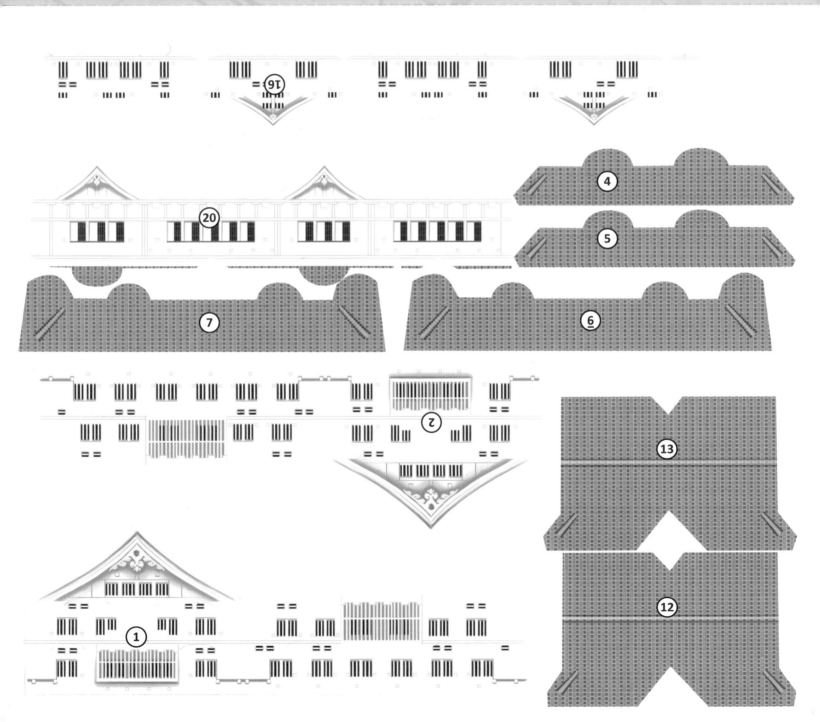

ST. PETER'S BASILICA

The Papal Basilica of St. Peter faces a vast keyhole-shaped public square, designed by Gian Lorenzo Bernini, which symbolizes the open arms of the Catholic Church and is capable of holding 100,000 people. Four rows of fine Doric columns of local travertine—300 in all—form an oval, 650 feet across, defined by three fountains and an Egyptian obelisk, which dates from the 13th century BC and was used as a turning post in the chariot races held at the Circus of Nero.

The dome is Michelangelo's architectural masterpiece.

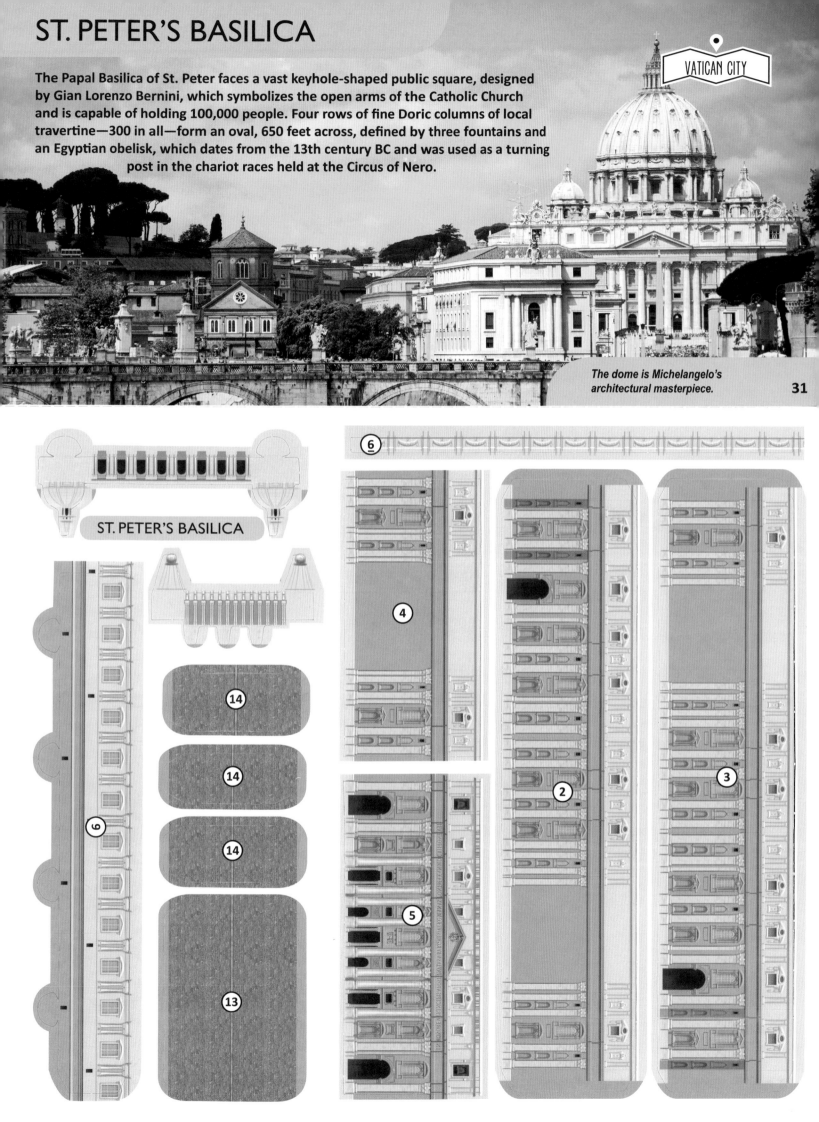

ST. PETER'S BASILICA

FEATURES:

- *Date of construction* 1506–1626
- *Height* 453 feet (dome of St. Peter's Basilica)
- *Size* 730 x 500 feet (internal area of St. Peter's Basilica), 877,500 square feet (St. Peter's Square)
- *Commissioners* Popes Julius II, Leo X, Clement VII, Paul III, Sixtus V, Gregory XIV, Clement VIII, Paul V, and Urban VII
- *Architects* Donato Bramante (master plan), Michelangelo, Giacomo della Porta (dome), Domenico Fontana (lantern), Carlo Maderno (west facade), Gian Lorenzo Bernini (square)
- *Material* Travertine
- *Purpose* Place of pilgrimage and worship

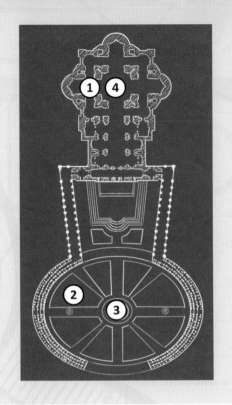

It is not something you could see as you walk in the square, but the resemblance of St. Peter's Basilica (1) and Square (2) to a key—the symbol of St. Peter—is too close to be anything but deliberate, and can be seen more closely in Bernini's plan for 1657. The obelisk at the center of the square (3) "balances" the overall design with the dome of the basilica (4).

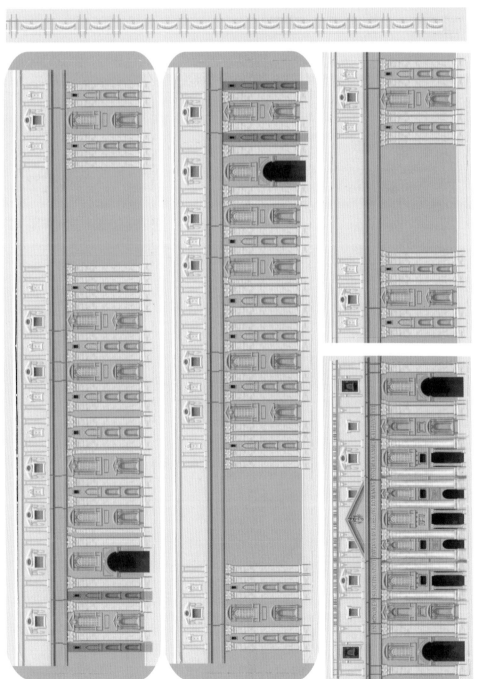

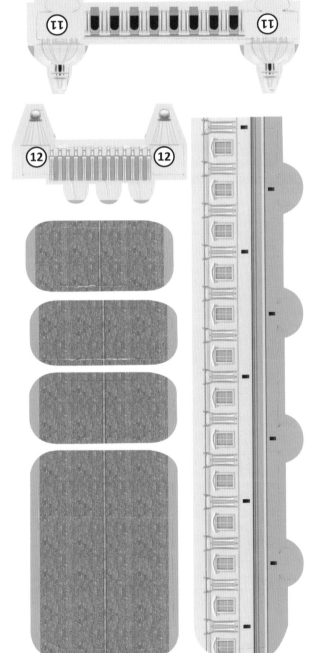

ARCHITECTURAL ELEMENTS

The basilica, with its dome designed by Michelangelo, is a fusion of Renaissance and Baroque styles. It was completed after the master's death by architect Giacomo della Porta, with the lantern designed by Domenico Fontana.

Strictly speaking, Michelangelo's "dome" is a paraboloid (not a hemisphere). It is supported by ribbing that rises out of the paired Corinthian columns, which act as buttresses that keep the dome from "bursting."

▲ *The columned hall in front of the basilica.*

◄ *Looking up at the richly painted ceiling of the basilica.*

► *A view of St. Peter's Square from the dome of the basilica.*

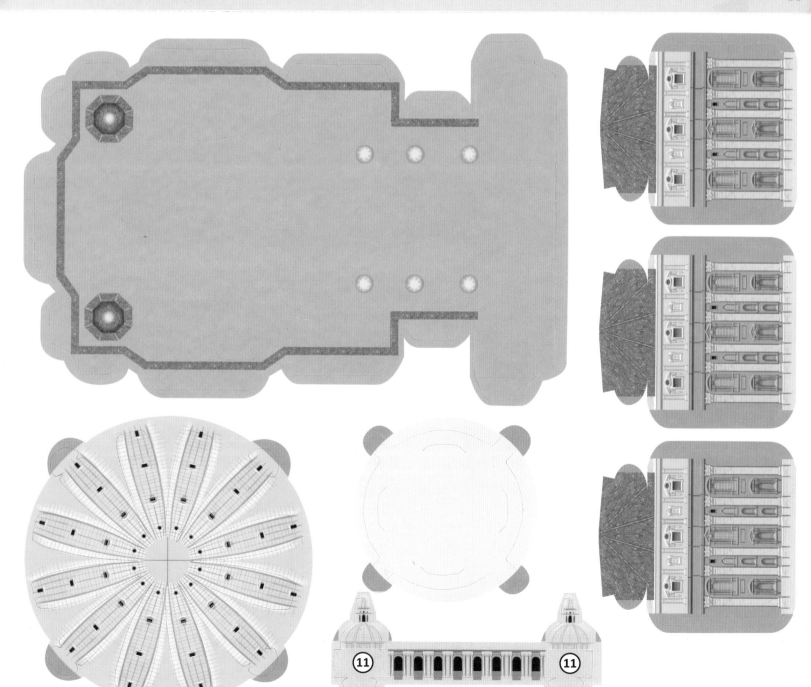

FASCINATING FACTS

• Since the ninth century, churches have acted as museums (as well as places of worship), commissioning and displaying the best works of art, including architecture, sculpture, and painting from the best practitioners in those fields. And at times when few people could read, they also acted as visual books for religious education.

• St. Peter's was the largest Christian church in the world, until it was beaten by a church in Yamoussoukro, Cote d'Ivoire, in 1989.

▲ *An 1897 etching from the Meyers Konversations-Lexikon.*

▶ *Statue of St. Peter with the key to St. Peter's Basilica.*

34

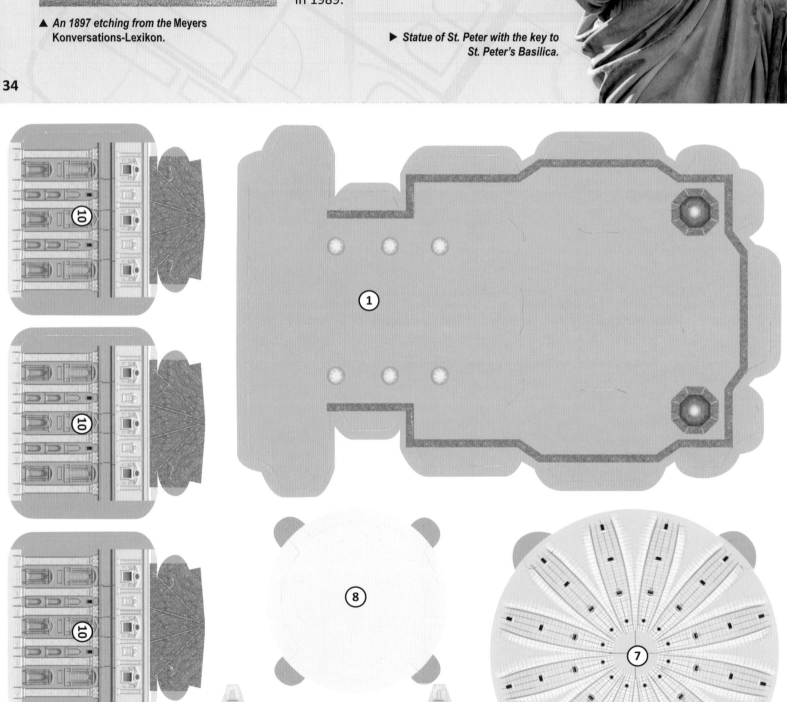

TAJ MAHAL

The Taj Mahal is the jewel in the crown of Muslim art in India, having been commissioned by the Mughal emperor Shah Jahan in memory of his favorite wife. The impact of the Taj Mahal, one of the Seven Wonders of the World, depends on its placing at the end of a water garden, rather than at its center. The perspective and the reflections add to the majesty of the architecture.

INDIA

The Taj Mahal, though in largely Hindu India, is a Muslim building.

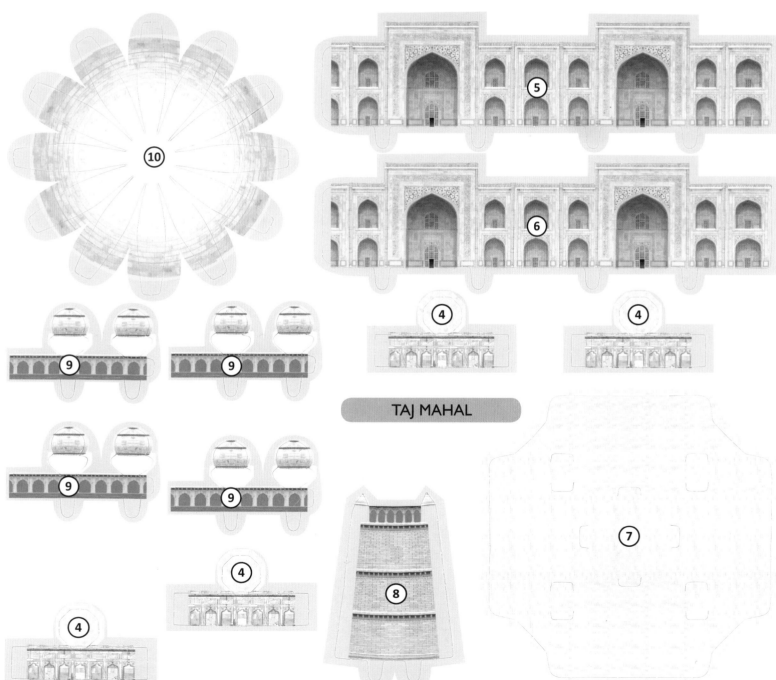

TAJ MAHAL

FEATURES:

- *Date of construction* 1631–1653

- *Height* 81 feet (tomb), 137 feet (minarets)

- *Size* 58 feet (diameter of the dome of the tomb), 42 acres (site)

- *Commissioner* Emperor Shah Jahan

- *Architect* Ustad Ahmad Lahauri

- *Materials* White marble and red sandstone

- *Purpose* Mausoleum, gateway, mosque, guesthouse, and bazaar

A cross section of the mausoleum of the Taj Mahal, showing the "onion" dome (1), and the burial chamber below (2). The long reverberation time in the mausoleum—for silence to be restored after a noise—is intended to suggest the idea of paradise, with the words of a prayer hanging in the air. The marble dome's height of 115 feet is, pleasingly, the same as the length of the base, and is accentuated as it sits on a cylindrical drum (3).

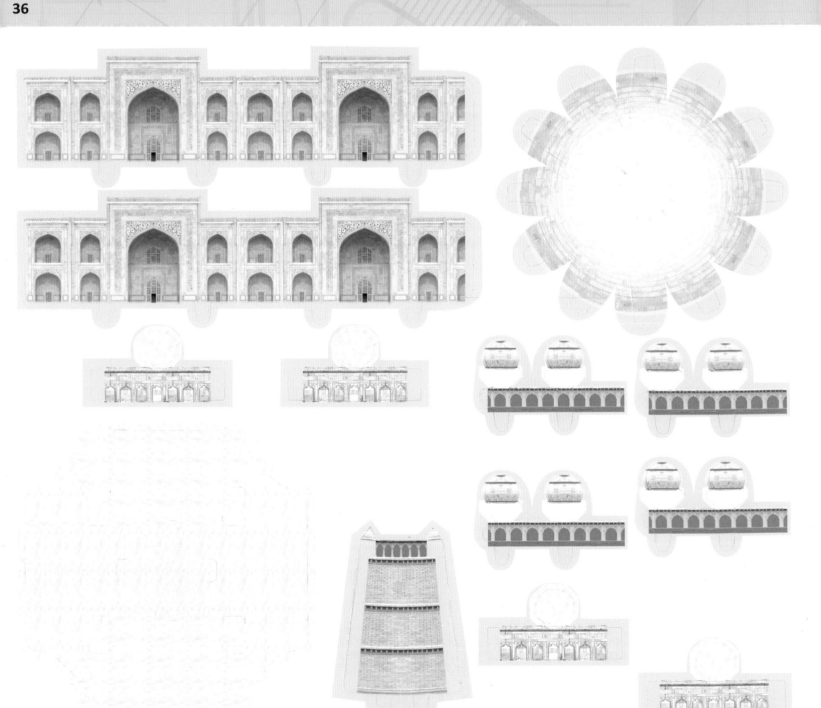

◀ *A close-up of one of the Taj Mahal's minarets.*

ARCHITECTURAL ELEMENTS

The key characteristics of the architecture, known as Shahjahan style, include its symmetry along two sides of a central axis, its curvilinear forms, new styles of columns, and plant motif decoration. The columns have a multifaceted shaft, with a capital (the topmost part) made up of small arches.

The plan is perfectly symmetrical: an octagonal tomb chamber in the center, surrounded by the portal halls and the four corner rooms.

▲ *A detail of the delicately carved marble walls of the Taj Mahal.*

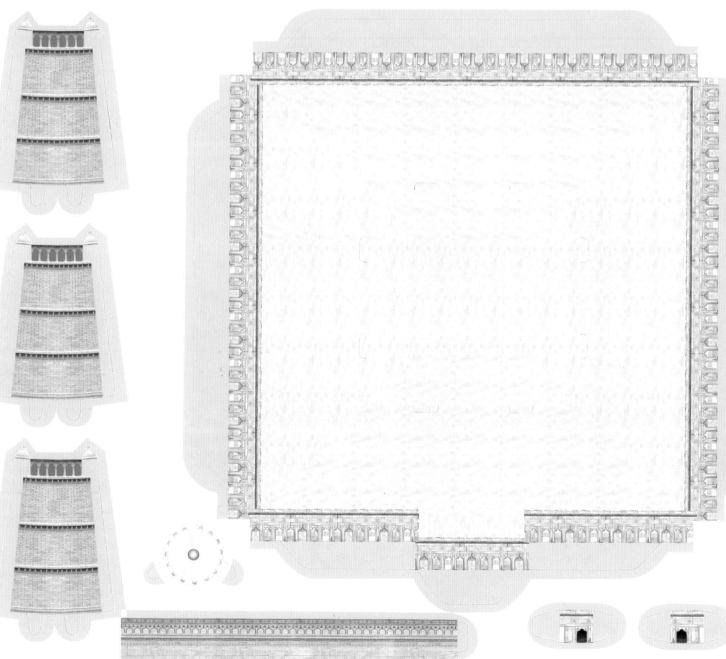

FASCINATING FACTS

• The Hindu text of the Vishnudharmottara Purana lays down the use of white stone for buildings for the Brahmins (priestly caste) and red for the Kshatriyas (warrior caste). This is reflected in the Taj Mahal by the white marble of the domes and the red sandstone used in the mosque and guesthouse.

• The reverberation time (the length of time sound echoes in the room) is 28 seconds. This is three times the length of the reverberation time in St. Peter's Basilica.

▲ A 1935 stamp featuring the Taj Mahal next to a portrait of the British king George V.

▶ A 19th-century engraving of the Taj Mahal.

38

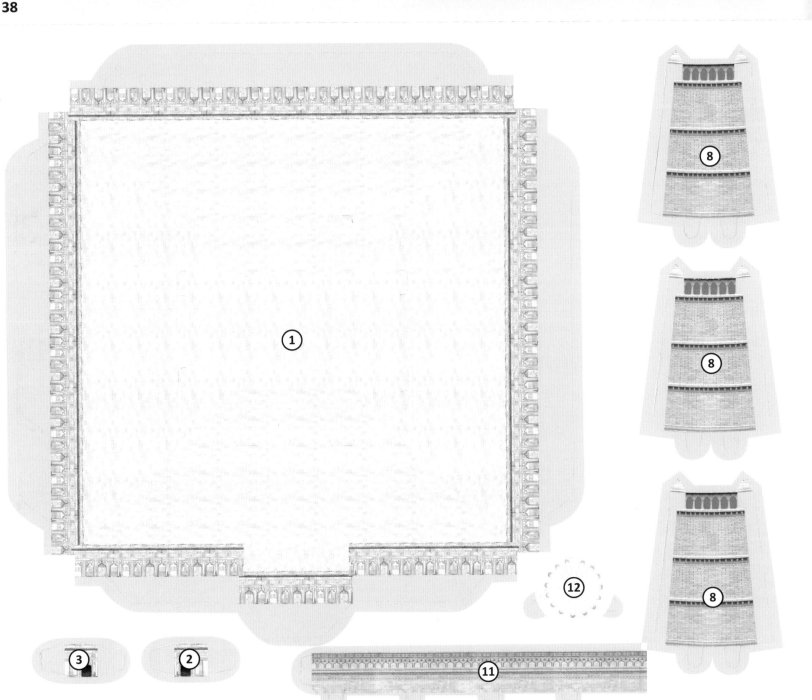

GREAT WALL OF CHINA

The Great Wall of China has served both strategic and social purposes over two millennia, protecting China's people and its culture from aggressors from the north. It also records all the advances in military, architectural, and engineering thinking over that period. The Great Wall begins at Shanhaiguan in the east and ends at Jiayuguan in the west—a straight-line distance of 1,200 miles. Apart from the wall itself, structures include watchtowers, fortresses, shelters, and horse tracks.

This is the longest wall in the world—by any measurement.

GREAT WALL OF CHINA

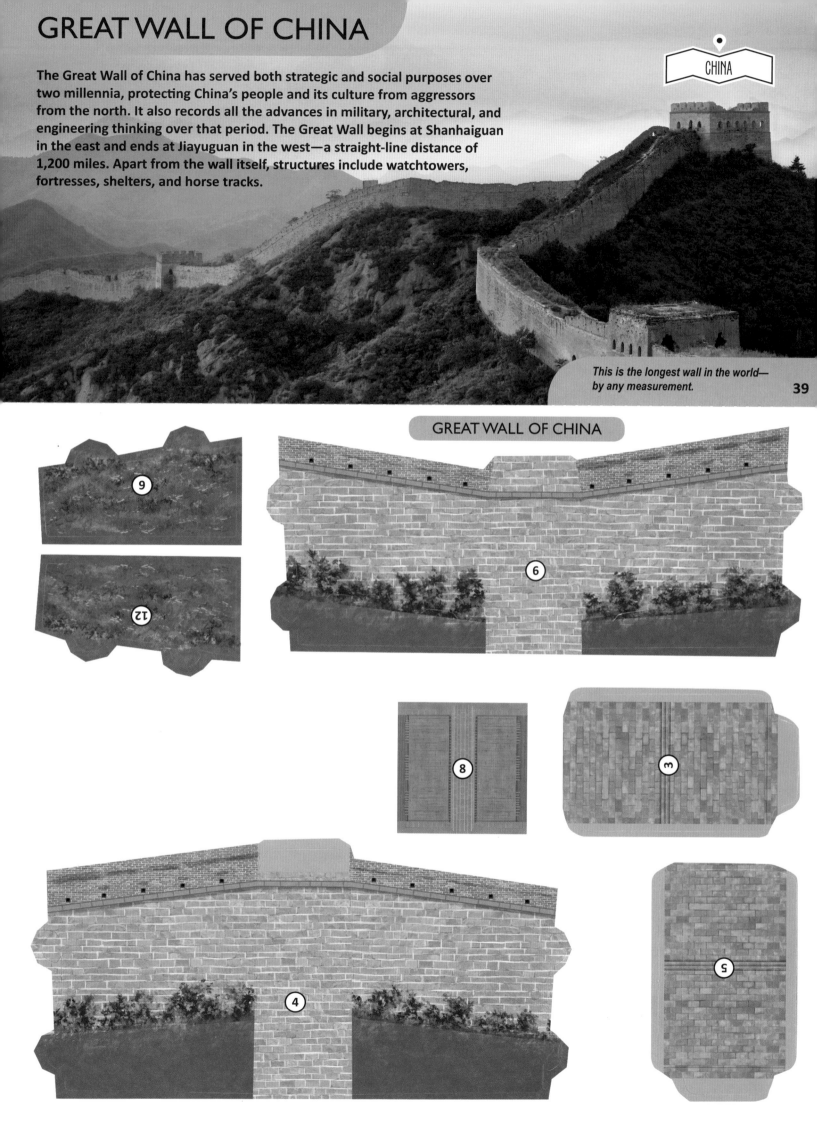

FEATURES:

- *Date of construction* 445 BC–AD 1664

- *Height* 16–26 feet

- *Length* 13,170 miles (total length of all wall ever built)

- *Commissioners* Warring states, Qin dynasty, Han dynasty, N. Wei dynasty, N. Qi/Sui dynasty, Liao/Jin dynasty, and Ming dynasty

- *Architect* Unknown

- *Materials* Earth, stone, and brick, according to eras and local conditions

- *Purpose* Defense

If you add together all the sections of the wall built between 445 BC and AD 1644, including all the overbuilding (additional sections, built parallel to existing walls), side branches, and natural barriers such as mountains and rivers, it comes to 13,170 miles. That's nearly five times the width of the United States, or almost halfway around the equator.

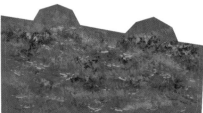

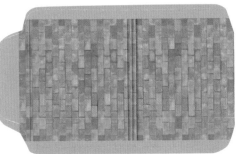

ARCHITECTURAL ELEMENTS

Of what remains today we can see that the Great Wall is a masterpiece of construction. It constitutes, on a continental scale, the world's finest example of the integration of architecture and landscape, and uses techniques ranging from the now partially fossilized rammed-earth fortifications dating from the Western Han period (206 BC–AD 9) to the superb masonry of the Ming period (1368–1644). Glutinous rice flour was used to bind the earliest bricks employed in its construction.

▲ The Great Wall of China close to Jinshanling, showing the watchtowers.

▶ An engraving on a section of the wall.

▶ A close-up of a ruined section of the wall.

A stamp printed in 1983 in China showing the Great Wall.

FASCINATING FACTS

• The answer to the question "How long is the Great Wall of China?" is like trying to describe the length of a piece of string—it's almost impossible to say. The Chinese still refer to it as the "10,000-Li Wall," with 10,000 li being about 3,100 miles. But that is the length it was as long ago as 206 BC.

An engraving from the 1890s. Note the number of visitors even then.

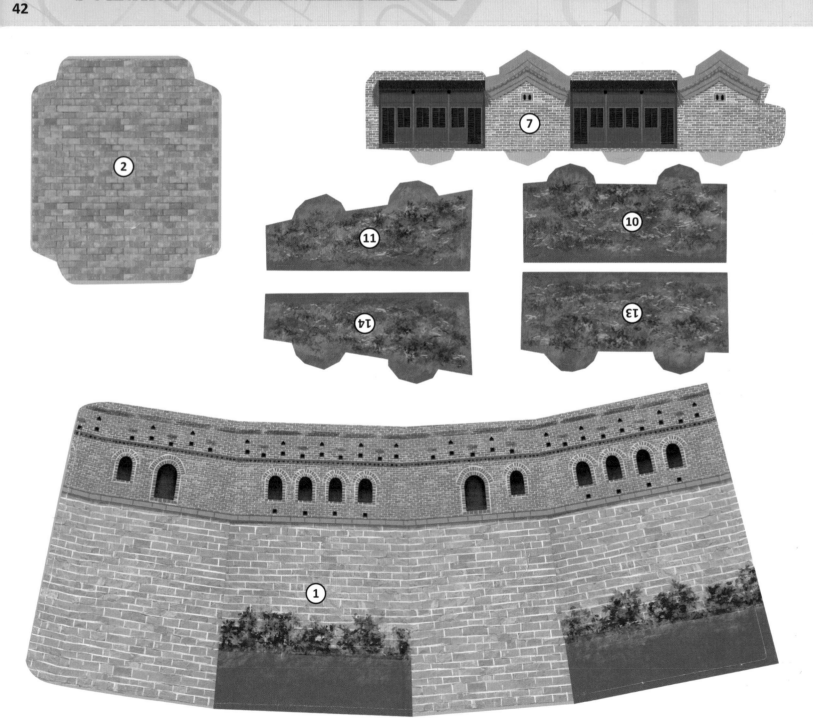

U.S. CAPITOL BUILDING

The U.S. Capitol in Washington, D.C., houses the chambers for the Senate in the north wing and the chambers for the House of Representatives in the south wing. It is an example of 19th-century neoclassical architecture, favored by Thomas Jefferson, and evokes the European ideals that guided the Founding Fathers of the new republic. None of the 17 plans submitted in an architecture competition were satisfactory, and the job was given to a late entrant, the British West Indian–born William Thornton, a trained medical doctor.

The building both symbolizes and accommodates American democracy.

43

U.S. CAPITOL BUILDING

FEATURES:

- *Date of construction* 1793–1868

- *Height* 288 feet (Rotunda), 180 feet (Statue of Freedom)

- *Size* 751 feet long; the Rotunda is 98 feet in diameter

- *Commissioner* President George Washington

- *Architects* Dr. William Thornton (1793–1803), Benjamin Henry Latrobe (1804–1817), Charles Bulfinch (1818–1829), Thomas U. Walter (1851–1864), Edward Clark (1864–1868)

- *Materials* Brick clad in marble and sandstone

- *Purpose* Home to the U.S. Senate and the House of Representatives, plus government buildings

William Thornton's original plan depicting a building composed of three sections. The central section (1) was topped by a low dome and flanked on the north (2) and south (3) by two rectangular wings, one for the Senate (4) and one for the House of Representatives (5). However, Jefferson had the idea for the Rotunda and ensured that it was built. President Washington commended the plan for its "grandeur, simplicity, and convenience."

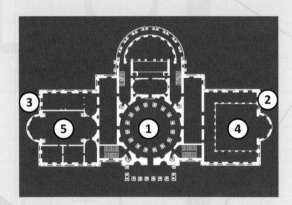

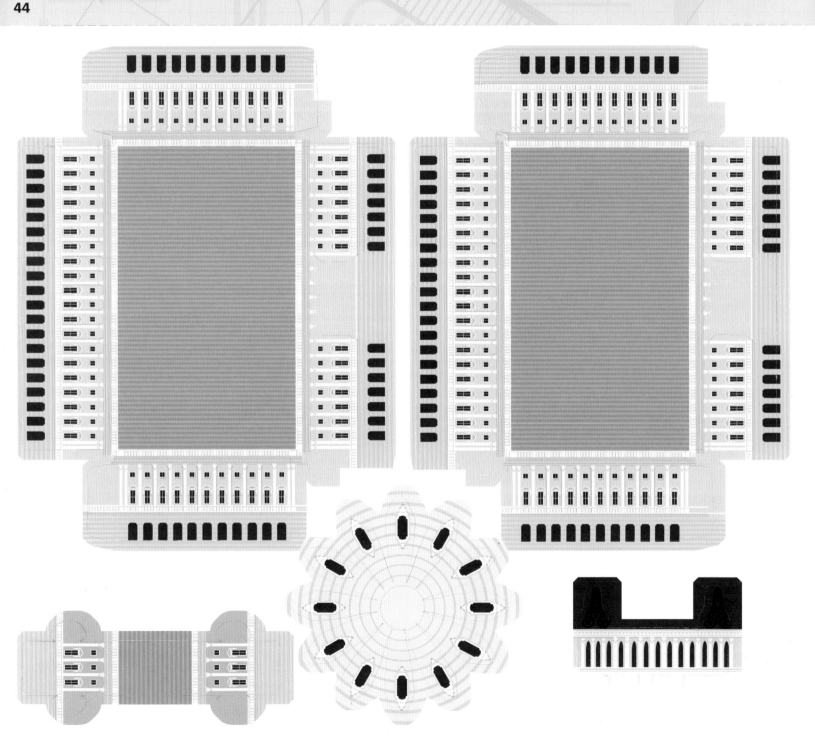

ARCHITECTURAL ELEMENTS

Renaissance architectural theorists laid down that the ground floor should be for servants. But Jefferson put the House and Senate chambers at ground level so the people could watch from public galleries.

In his designs for the old Supreme Court chamber, Latrobe invented a new American order of architecture (to follow Ionic, Doric, and Corinthian), incorporating corncob and tobacco leaves at the tops of columns.

▶ *Cupola and ceiling of the Rotunda of the Capitol Building.*

▲ *Latrobe incorporated tobacco leaves at the tops of the columns.*

45

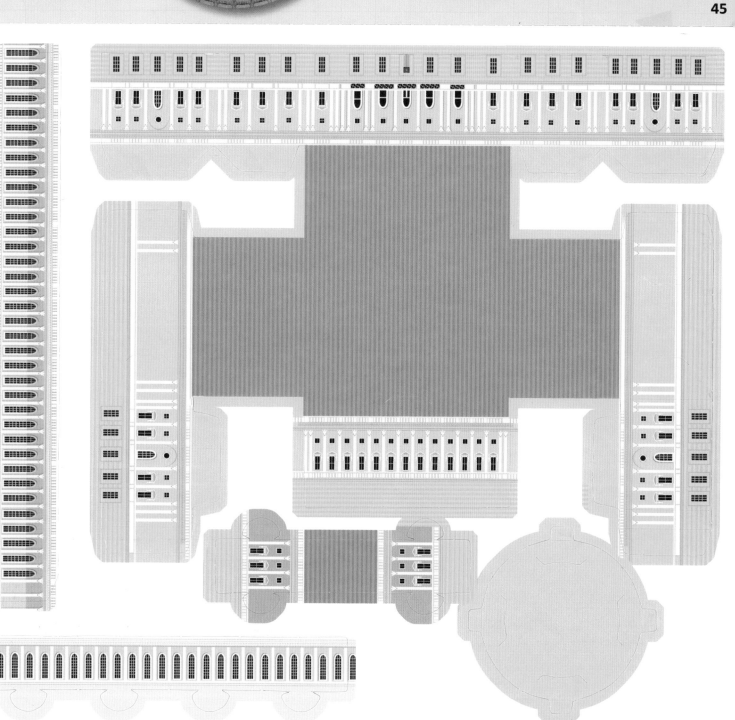

FASCINATING FACTS

• Visitors commonly ask "Who is buried in the crypt?" The answer is no one—it was designed for George Washington, but he preferred to be buried at Mount Vernon.

• On August 24, 1814, during the War of 1812, British troops set fire to the building. Architect Latrobe took this opportunity to make changes to the building's interior design and to introduce new materials, such as marble, instead of the soft sandstone used in the first phases.

▲ *A cartoon of the burning of the Capitol by the British in 1814.*

▶ *An 1814 watercolor of the damaged shell of the Capitol after burning by the British.*

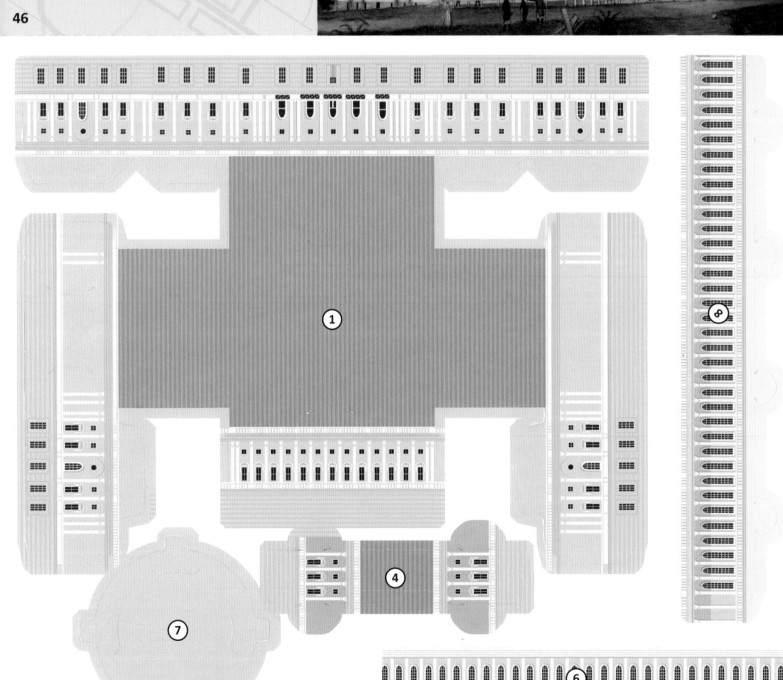

THE WHITE HOUSE

"The White House" has long been used to describe the administration of the U.S. president. But it is also a building and, despite British attempts to burn it down in 1814, is still recognizably the one designed by Irish-born architect James Hoban and opened in 1800. The West Wing was added in 1901, during Theodore Roosevelt's time, to house the offices. The East Wing was added for social events in 1948.

The White House is the symbol of the presidency of the United States.

47

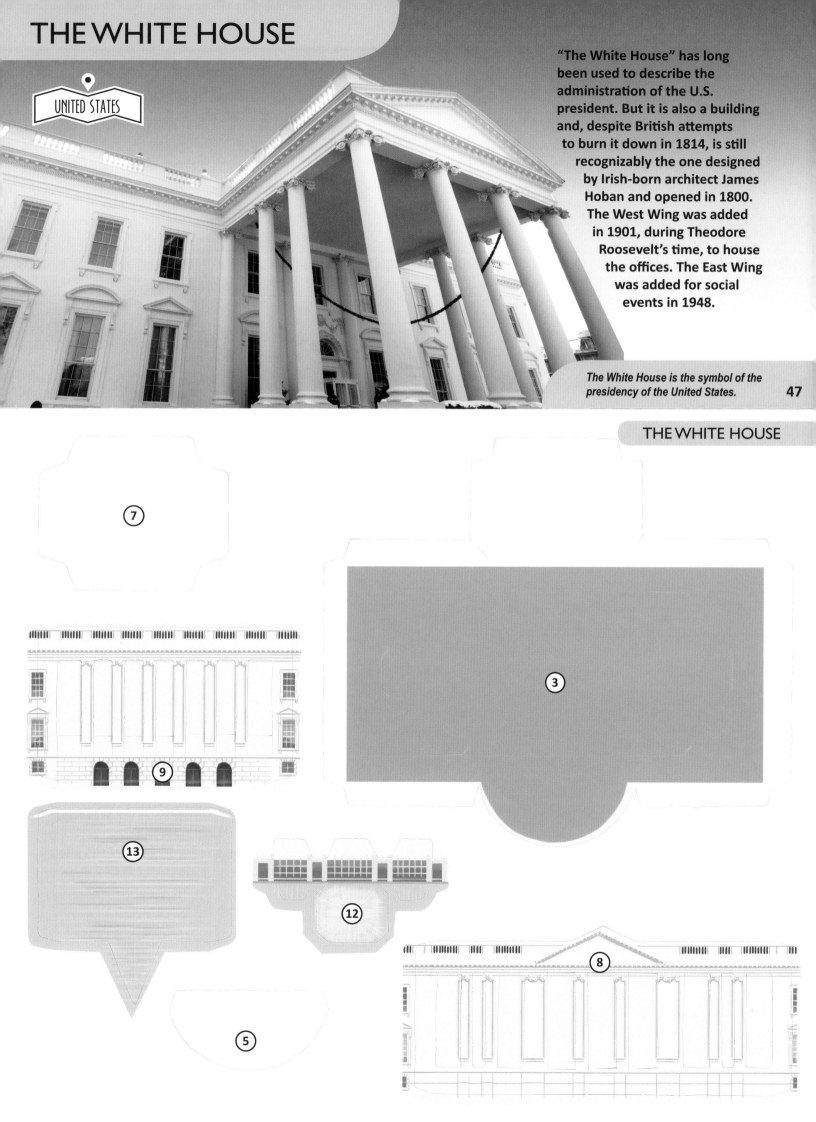

FEATURES:

- *Date of construction* 1792–1800

- *Height* 70 feet on north side, 60 feet on south side

- *Size* 168 x 152 feet (with porticos), with a total floor area over the six floors of 55,000 square feet

- *Commissioner* President George Washington

- *Architect* James Hoban

- *Materials* Sandstone (with a whitewash of lime, rice glue, casein, and lead) and brick

- *Purpose* President's residence and offices

The main floor plan of James Hoban's "Executive Mansion" shows the simple domesticity of the design: a vestibule (1) and corridor (2) with the main rooms leading off. The Green Room (3), the oval-shaped Blue Room (4), and the Red Room (5) all overlook the South Portico (6) and are all still recognizable today. The East Room (7) is still the largest room in the White House and has been used for everything from receptions and bill-signing ceremonies to boxing and wrestling matches (in President Theodore Roosevelt's day).

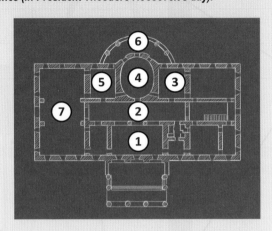

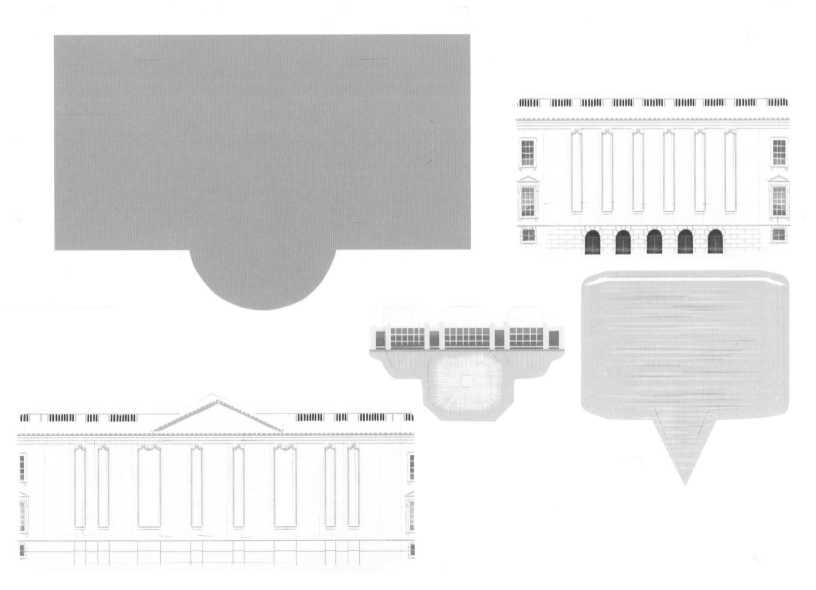

▼ *Interior of the White House showing the Oval Office and the president's desk.*

▲ *The White House has been the official residence of every president of the United States since 1800.*

ARCHITECTURAL ELEMENTS

Hoban's building is Palladian in style—after the Italian Renaissance architect Palladio. Its direct influences include a number of Irish country houses, and Leinster House in Dublin, which later became home to the Irish parliament. A further inspiration was Château de Rastignac, France, by Mathurin Salat, which Thomas Jefferson had visited.

Although by no means modest, there is an understated grandeur to the White House, in keeping with its still primary function as a home.

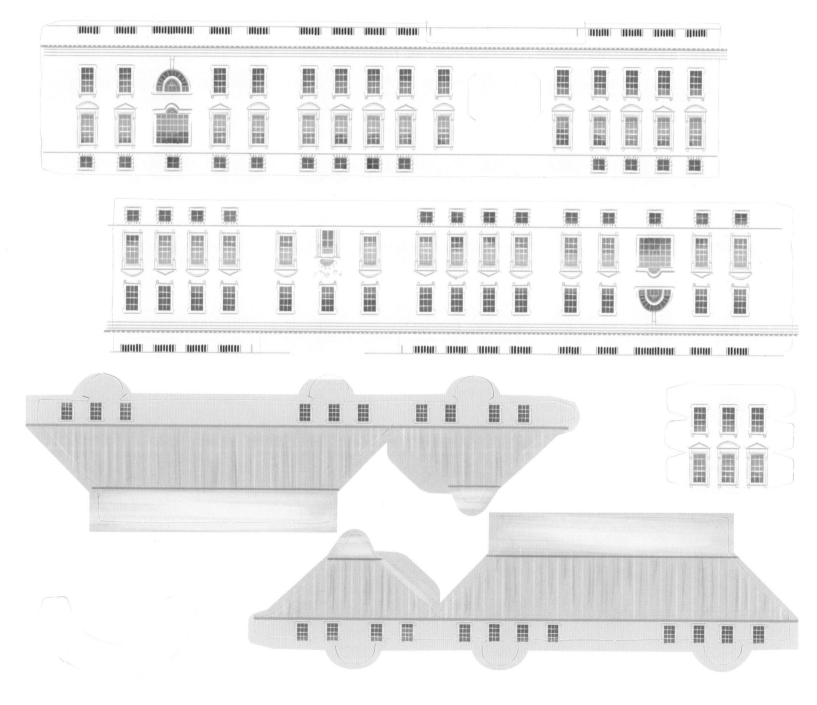

FASCINATING FACTS

• The Oval Office, designed by Nathan C. Wyeth for President William Howard Taft, is shaped so that a circle of guests could be introduced to the president.

• Above the mantelpiece in the state dining room is an inscription taken from a letter by President John Adams to his wife. It reads: "I Pray Heaven To Bestow the Best of Blessings on This house and All that shall hereafter Inhabit it. May none but Honest and Wise Men ever rule under This Roof."

The West Wing under construction in 1934, commissioned by Franklin D. Roosevelt and designed by Eric Gugler.

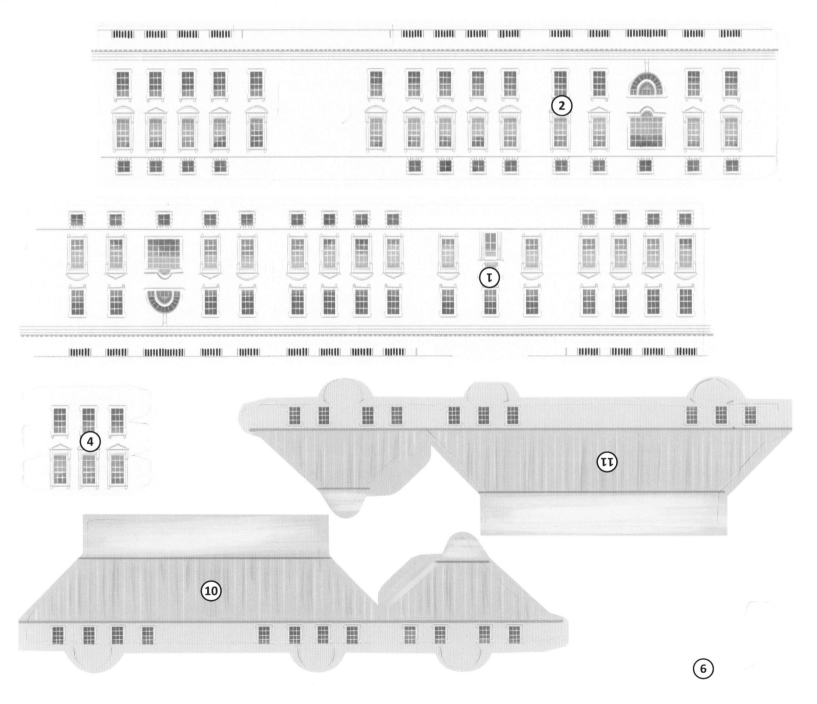

HOUSES OF PARLIAMENT

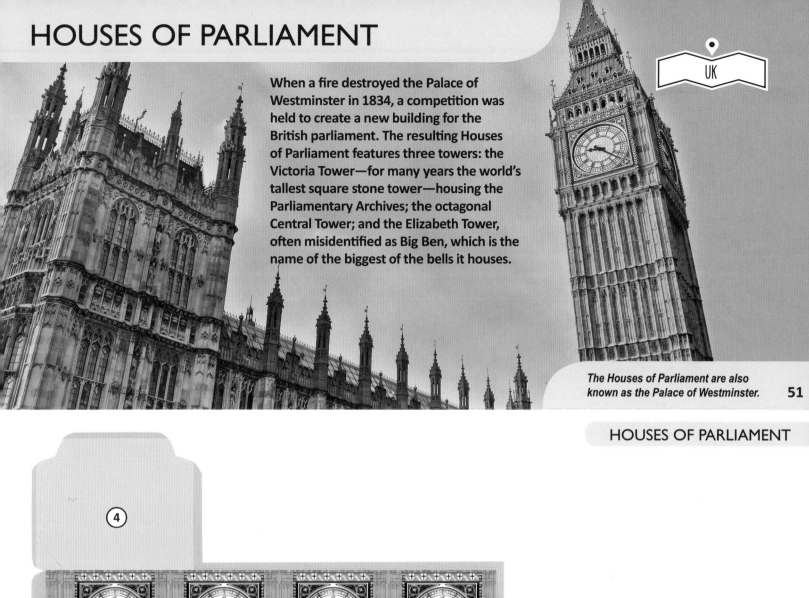

When a fire destroyed the Palace of Westminster in 1834, a competition was held to create a new building for the British parliament. The resulting Houses of Parliament features three towers: the Victoria Tower—for many years the world's tallest square stone tower—housing the Parliamentary Archives; the octagonal Central Tower; and the Elizabeth Tower, often misidentified as Big Ben, which is the name of the biggest of the bells it houses.

The Houses of Parliament are also known as the Palace of Westminster.

51

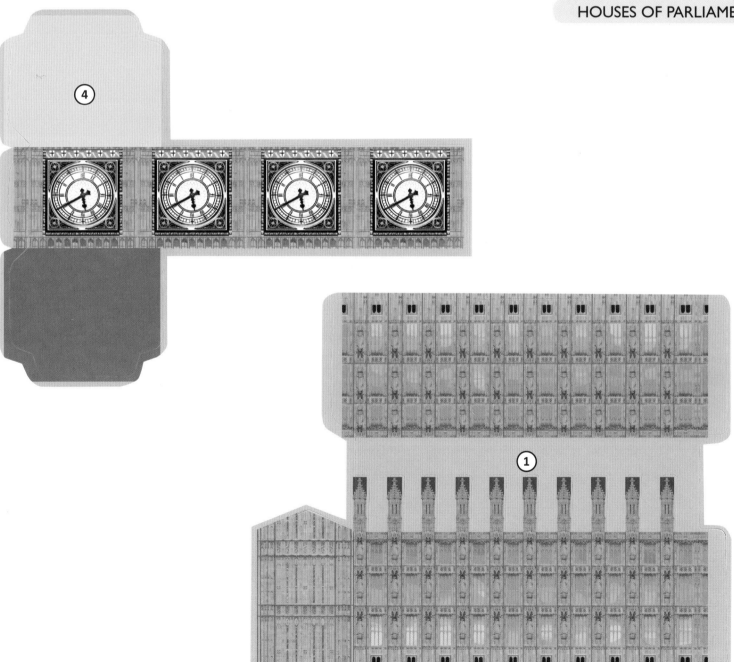

FEATURES:

- *Date of construction* 1840–1870
- *Height* 323 feet (Victoria Tower), 300 feet (Central Tower), 316 feet (Elizabeth Tower)
- *Size* 8 acres (whole site)
- *Commissioner* The Royal Commission
- *Architect* Charles Barry, with Augustus Welby Pugin
- *Materials* Anston limestone, Cornish granite, and cast iron
- *Purpose* Home to the House of Commons and the House of Lords

The Elizabeth Tower, which stands at the north end of the Houses of Parliament, was completed in 1859; the Great Clock started on May 31, and the Great Bell's strikes were heard for the first time on July 11.

Inside the tower, a staircase of 334 steps climbs to the belfry. The shaft of the tower is so narrow that when they were winching the bells into place, the biggest one, Big Ben, had to be turned on its side to fit through it. A pile of sandbags is placed at the bottom of the shaft to reduce the damage should any of the weights or bells fall. As well as being a working building, the tower provides London with one of its most famous landmarks.

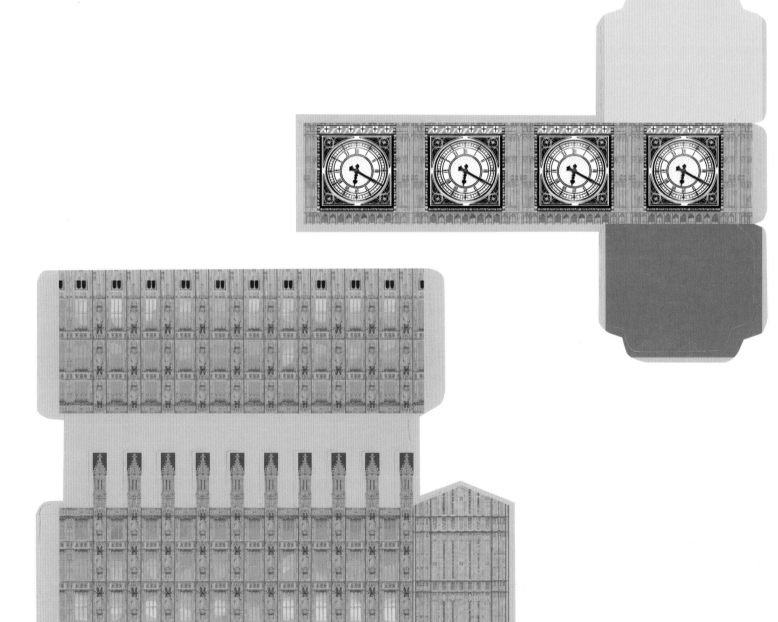

ARCHITECTURAL DETAILS

The controversy over the design of the Houses of Parliament epitomized the Battle of Styles between the Classical and the Gothic. Barry's first design was Classical, but partly under the influence of his pupil Pugin, the completed design was decidedly Gothic—the interiors are among the finest examples of Gothic Revival. However, the Gothic purist Pugin did not consider the design Gothic at all, remarking to a friend, "All Grecian, sir; Tudor details on a classic body."

The equestrian statue of King Richard I in Old Palace Yard.

◄ *A detail of the Victoria Tower, the largest and tallest tower of the Palace of Westminster.*

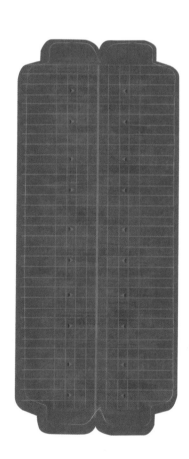

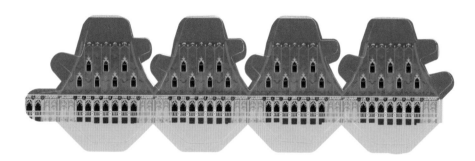

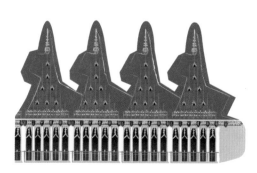

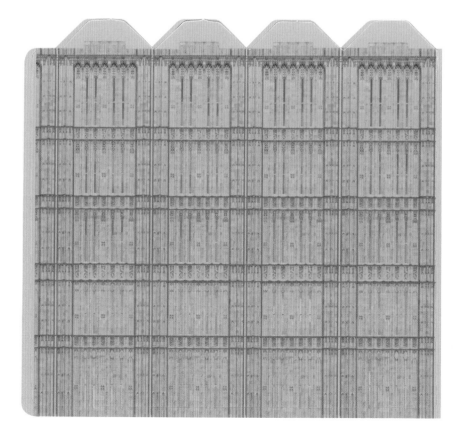

FASCINATING FACTS

• An earlier plan to redesign Parliament was made by William Kent in the 1730s. Kent's plans show a white Portland stone building, almost as big as the famous Hall of Mirrors at Versailles, with Corinthian columns and Venetian windows—a style that typified 18th-century architecture. However, we would not have been able to enjoy it today, as it would have been consumed by the fire of 1834.

◀ *A drawing of the unbuilt parliament building by William Kent from the 1730s.*

▶ *Interior of Westminster Hall, the oldest part of the Palace of Westminster.*

54

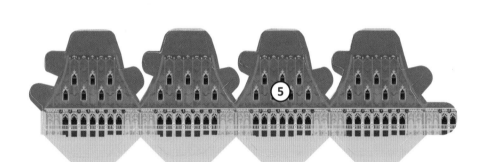

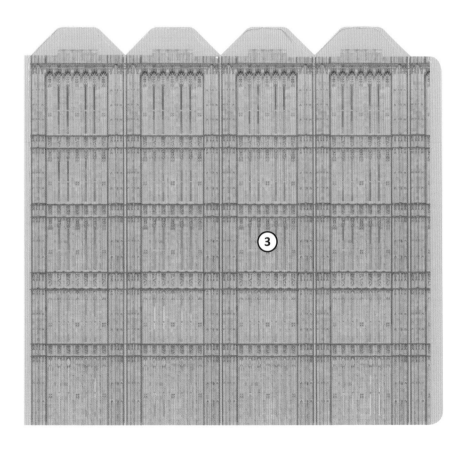

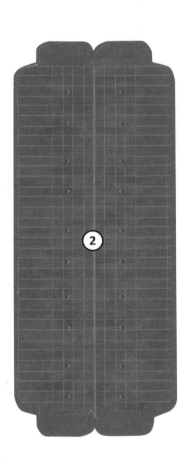

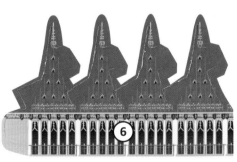

NEUSCHWANSTEIN CASTLE

Neuschwanstein Castle is the finest architectural example of myth fulfillment. Inspired by Wagner's operas *Tannhäuser* and *Lohengrin*, Ludwig II of Bavaria had a set designer working with an architect to realize his fantasy castle. Having lost a war to Prussia, he was no longer a sovereign ruler; the fantasy was now his only kingdom.

Neuschwanstein is a fantasy castle made real.

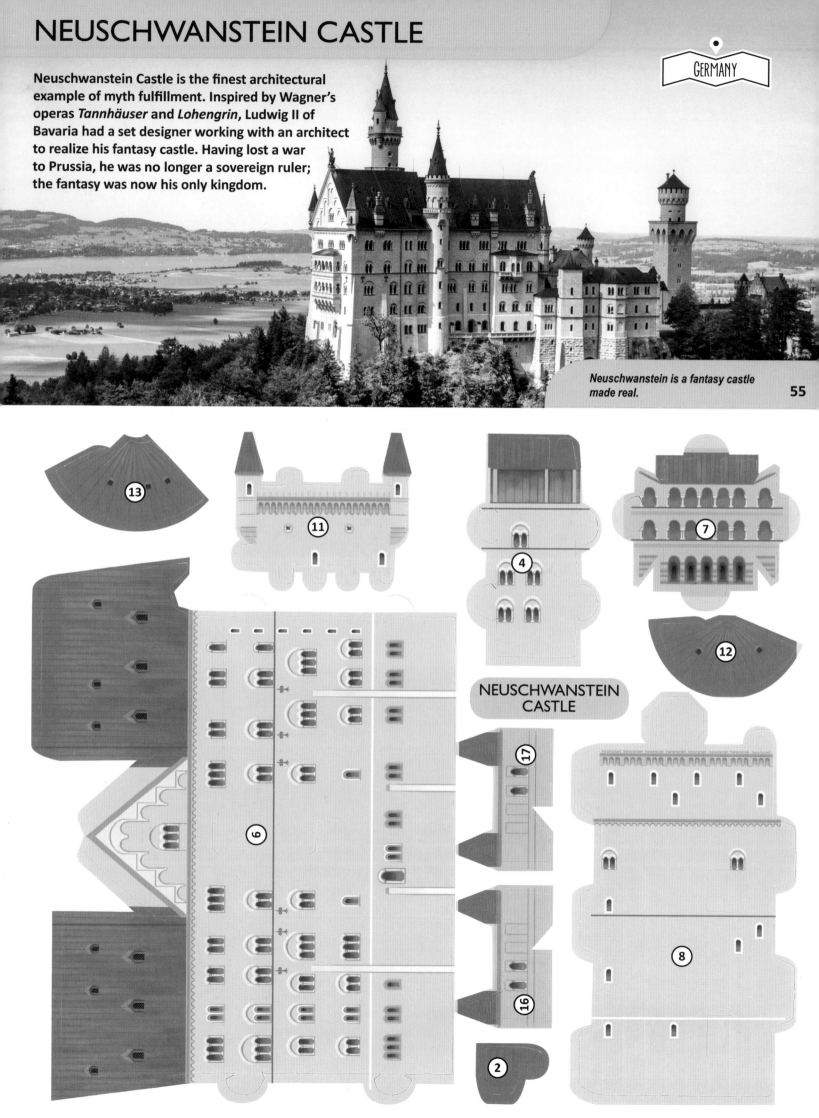

NEUSCHWANSTEIN CASTLE

FEATURES:

- *Date of construction* 1864–1880

- *Height* 213 feet (northern tower)

- *Size* 89 x 33 feet (Hall of Singers), 66 x 39 feet (Throne Hall), 8,500 square feet (overall castle)

- *Commissioner* King Ludwig II of Bavaria

- *Architects* Christian Jank (set designer), Eduard Riedel (architect, realization)

- *Materials* White limestone, sandstone brick, Salzburg marble, and steel frame (for the Throne Hall)

- *Purpose* Residential

Ground floor plan of the castle, showing the foundations of a massive tower that was never built (1). This is what is called a "cranked" plan, with part of the building set at a different angle to the rest—here two staircase towers act as pivots (2). These lead up to the Throne Room (3), which occupies the second and third floors and the entire west section of the building. It was inspired by Byzantine churches, such as the All Saints Court Church in Munich.

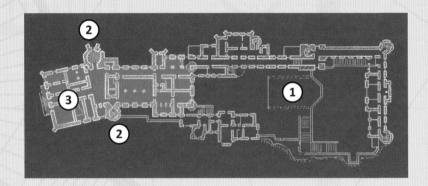

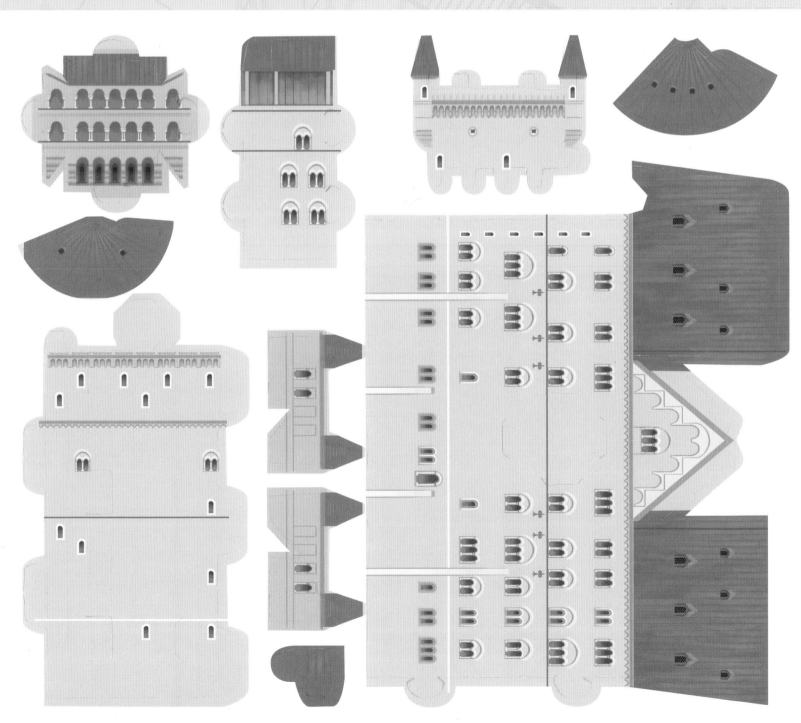

ARCHITECTURAL ELEMENTS

The style was intended to be neo-Gothic, but the results are better classified as Romanesque Revival. The rounded arches of the Romanesque style mix with the pointed arches and slender towers of the Gothic. The Byzantine also puts in an appearance, in the decor of the Throne Hall. And underpinning it all is the advanced technology of the 19th century, in the construction and servicing of the castle.

◄ *One of the lavish interiors of the romantic castle.*

▶ *The castle with its backdrop of cloud.*

57

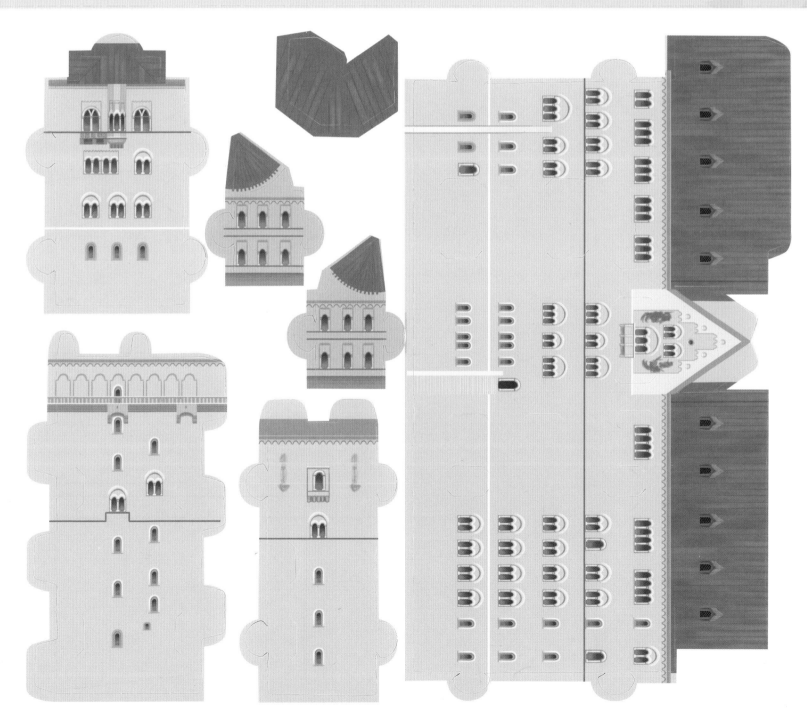

FASCINATING FACTS

• Just 19 years after the first performance of Richard Wagner's romantic fantasy opera *Tannhäuser*, and 14 years after the German composer created the part of the Swan Knight in *Lohengrin*, Ludwig commissioned his own fairy-tale castle and dubbed it New Swan Stone, or Neuschwanstein, after the Swan Knight—a classic example of life imitating art.

▲ *The cobbled courtyard of Neuschwanstein Castle.*

▶ *A stamp showing the Bavarian Alps and Neuschwanstein Castle.*

▲ *The fairy-tale towers of Neuschwanstein seen from above.*

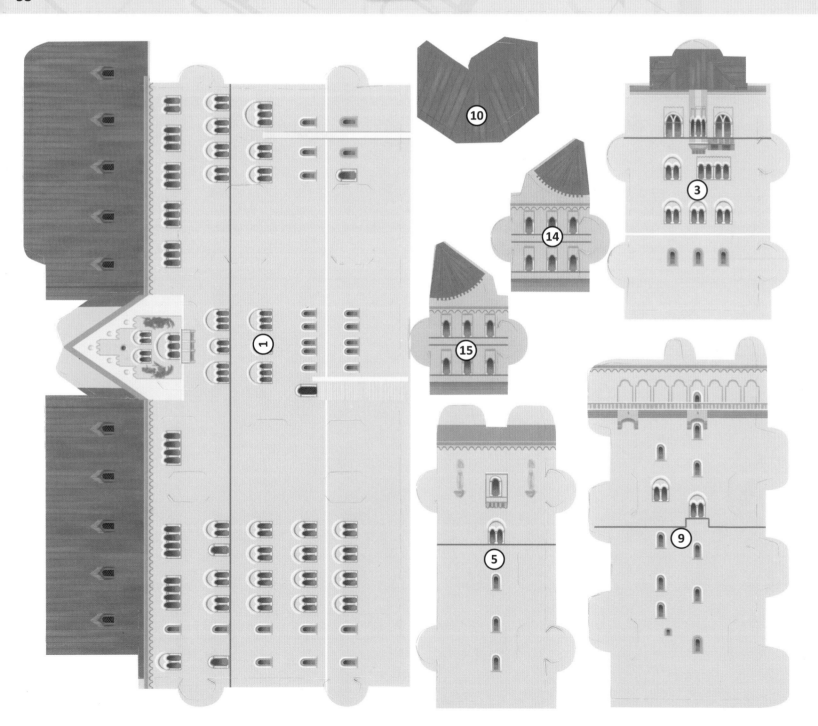

STATUE OF LIBERTY

New York's Statue of Liberty symbolizes America's welcoming spirit toward immigrants. The words of a sonnet written in 1883 by Emma Lazarus, a Jewish American writer, are engraved on the plinth:

Give me your tired, your poor,
Your huddled masses yearning to
*   breathe free,*
The wretched refuse of your teeming
*   shore.*
Send these, the homeless, tempest-
*   tossed, to me:*
I lift my lamp beside the golden door.

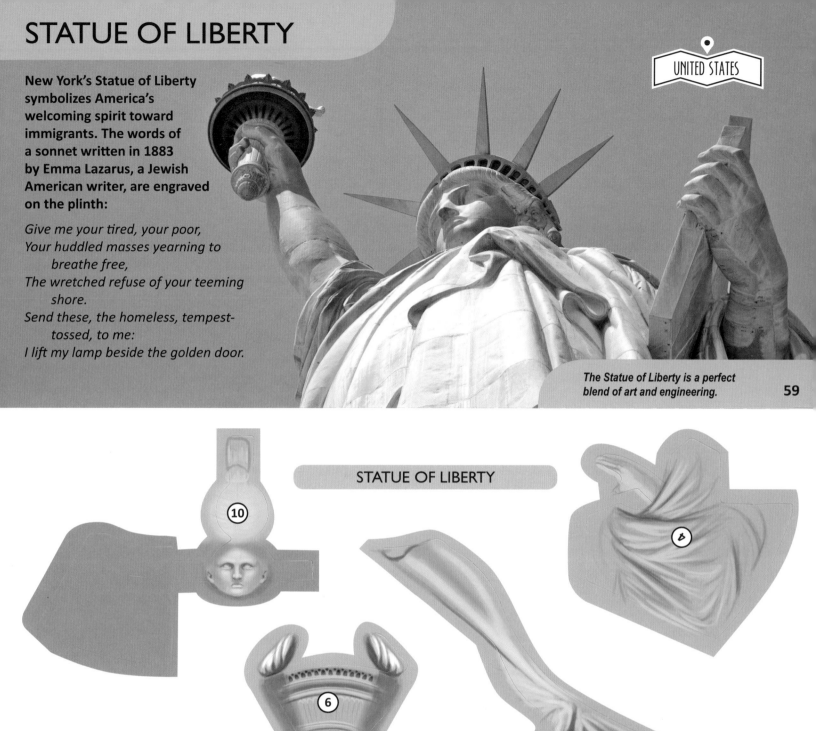

The Statue of Liberty is a perfect blend of art and engineering.

59

STATUE OF LIBERTY

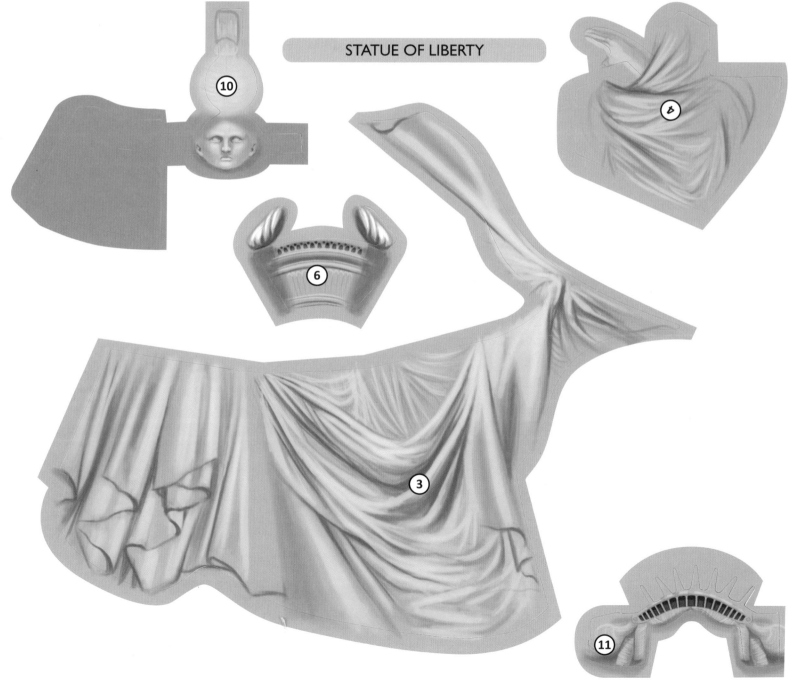

FEATURES:

- *Date of construction* 1886
- *Height* 305 feet
- *Commissioner* Édouard de Laboulaye
- *Architect* Frédéric Auguste Bartholdi, in collaboration with engineer Gustave Eiffel
- *Materials* Copper with wrought-iron strapwork (replaced by stainless steel in 1986)
- *Purpose* Symbol of liberty, fraternity, and tolerance

A cross section of the statue, showing the lattice (crisscrossed framework) of the iron structure. With no computers to aid him, French designer Gustave Eiffel had to figure out how to re-create the human form manually, and it took hundreds of drawings to get it right. The statue was transported in pieces to the United States and erected without the use of scaffolding, with all the construction materials hoisted up by steam-driven cranes.

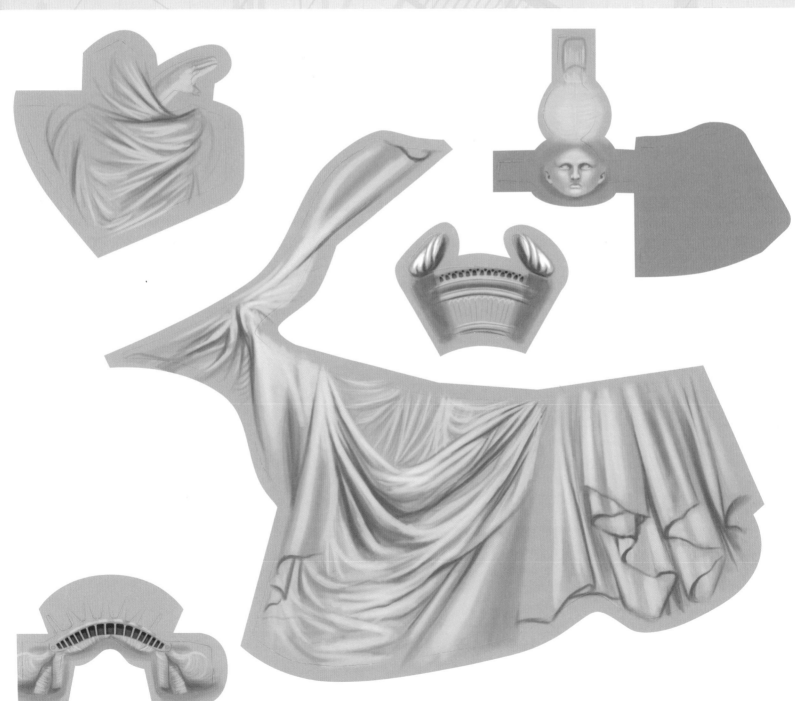

ARCHITECTURAL ELEMENTS

Standing on a pedestal designed by American architect Richard Morris Hunt, the statue was conceived by French author and antislavery campaigner Édouard de Laboulaye, and realized by two other Frenchmen: architect Frédéric Auguste Bartholdi and engineer Gustave Eiffel, who designed the columns for the backbone, and whose tower in Paris opened just three years later. Lady Liberty is very thin-skinned—the copper is less than a tenth of an inch thick.

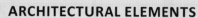

◄ *A close-up of Lady Liberty.*

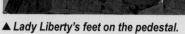

▲ *Lady Liberty's feet on the pedestal.*

The Statue of Liberty— the first glimpse of the New World for countless immigrants.

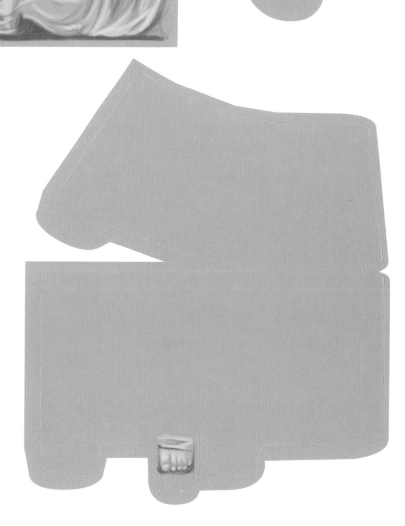

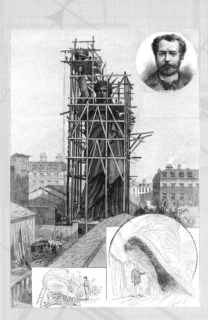

FASCINATING FACTS

• The statue's arm and torch were on display for six years in Madison Square Garden, in order to raise the money to erect it—the costs of its manufacture were a gift of the French people.

• The Statue of Liberty was far too big to be transported in one piece; instead it arrived as 350 pieces in 214 packing crates. Fortunately, it came with an instruction manual.

▲ An 1884 engraving of the construction, showing the statue and a portrait of Frédéric Bartholdi.

► The right arm of the statue on display in Madison Square Garden prior to assembly.

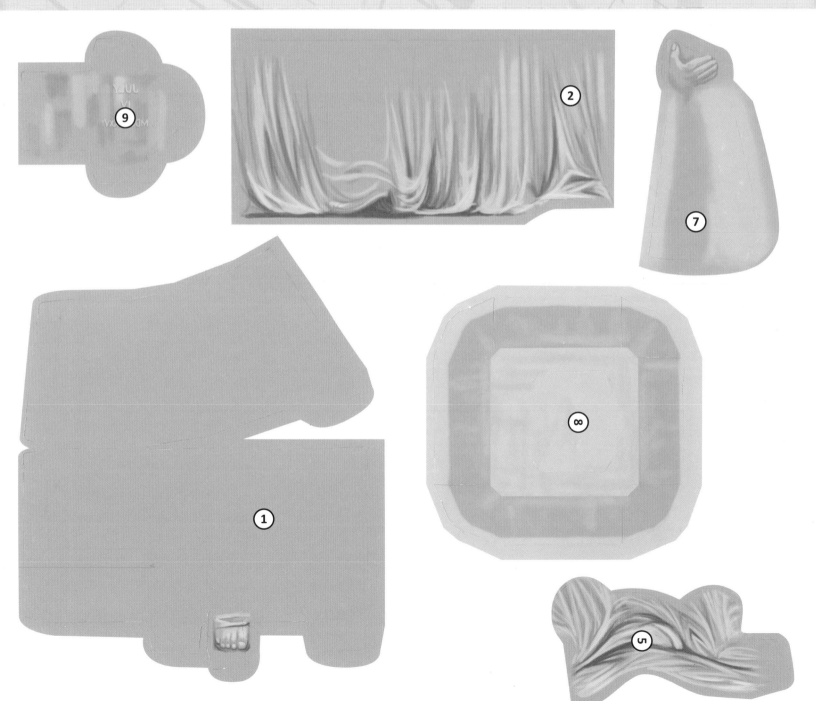

EIFFEL TOWER

The Eiffel Tower was designed by the French engineer Gustave Eiffel for the 1889 Exposition Universelle. The lifts were not ready in time, so the first 132,000 visitors—during its first 11 days—climbed the 1,710 steps of the world's tallest man-made structure to gain an unprecedented view of Paris. People were desperate to take in the view over Paris previously seen only by a handful of hot-air ballooners (the airplane had yet to be invented).

It was the world's tallest structure at the time of its construction.

63

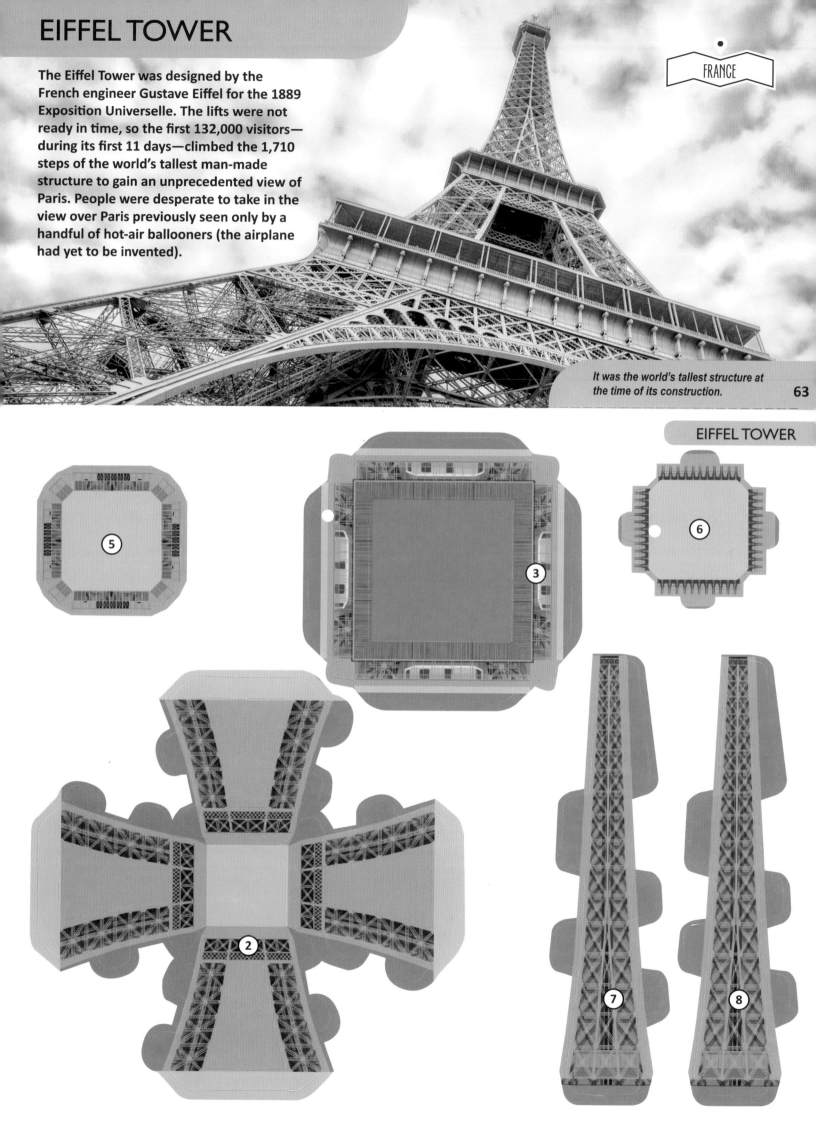

EIFFEL TOWER

FEATURES:

- *Date of construction* 1889
- *Height* 984 feet (1,063 feet including antenna)
- *Size* 410 x 410 feet
- *Commissioners* Maurice Koechlin and Émile Nouguier
- *Engineer* Gustave Eiffel
- *Material* Iron
- *Purpose* Exhibit, tourist attraction, and communications tower

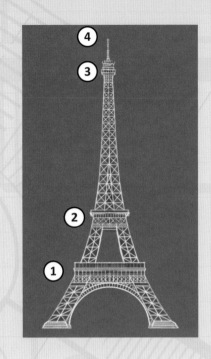

This drawing of the Eiffel Tower shows the dimensions of its platforms and stages.

On the first platform (1), at 186 feet above the ground, there are shops, restaurants, exhibitions, and a section with a glass floor.

The second platform (2), at 380 feet, has similar facilities but better views.

The third and top platform (3) (906 feet) still provides some of the best views of Paris.

The very tip of the tower (4), including its radio mast, is at 1,063 feet—the height of an 81-story building.

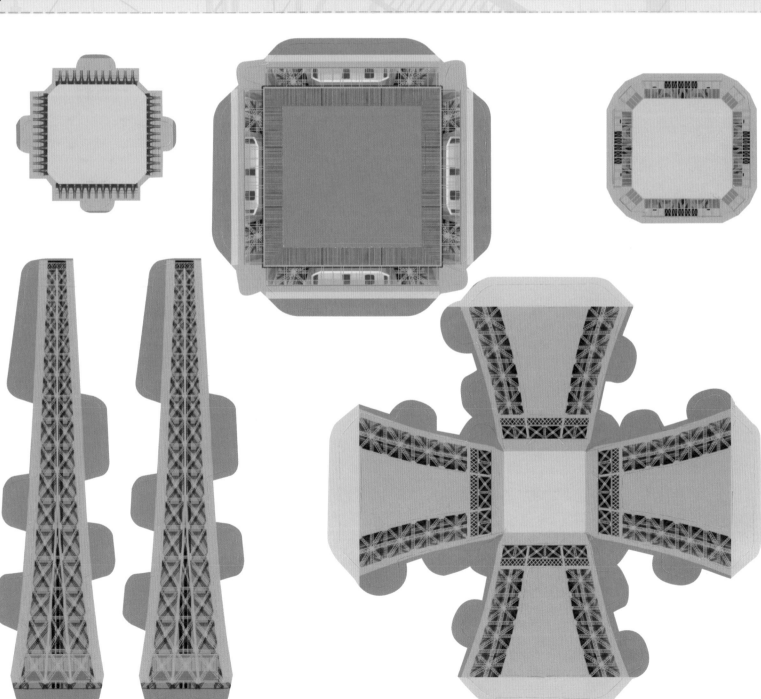

ARCHITECTURAL ELEMENTS

To mark the centenary of the French Revolution, the French government planned the Exposition Universelle in Paris and held a design competition for a monument to be built on the Champ-de-Mars. The Centennial Committee chose Gustave Eiffel's design of an open-lattice, wrought-iron tower from a hundred entries.

Eiffel's bridges can be seen in Portugal, Spain, Hungary, Egypt, Vietnam, and Chile, as well as in France. He also designed the framework of the recently erected Statue of Liberty.

▲ A few of the 2.5 million rivets it took to build the Eiffel Tower.

▲ A view looking straight up the Eiffel Tower from its base.

▶ Detail of the intricate iron latticework.

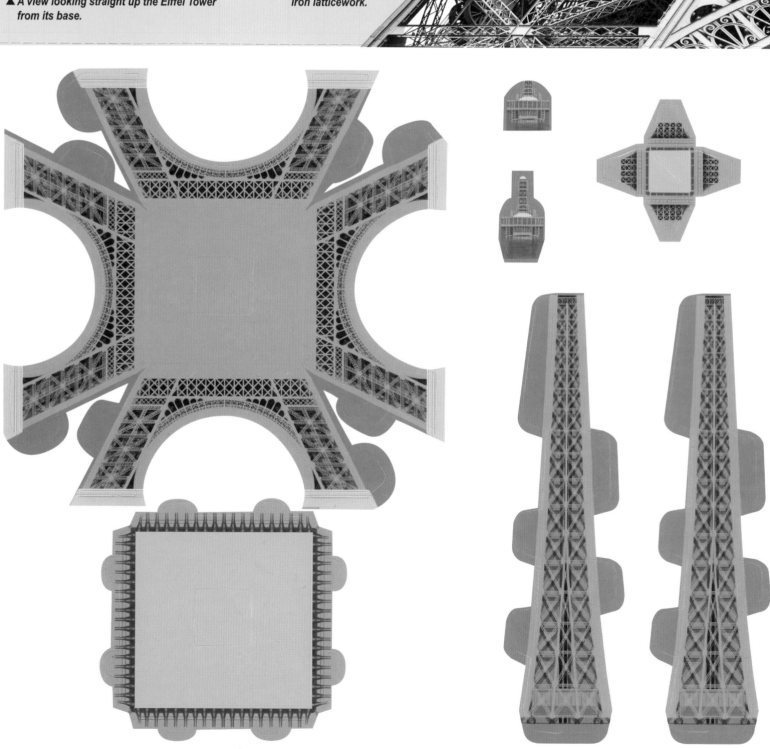

FASCINATING FACTS

• Responding to critics who described his tower as an eyesore, Eiffel replied, "Do people think that because we are engineers, beauty plays no part in what we build, that if we aim for the solid and lasting, we don't do our utmost to achieve elegance?"

• The Eiffel Tower's planned life span was just 20 years, after which it was to be demolished. A public change of heart—and its use in the development of radio communications—assured its longevity.

◀ *A hand-tinted picture postcard of the 1900 Exposition Universelle.*

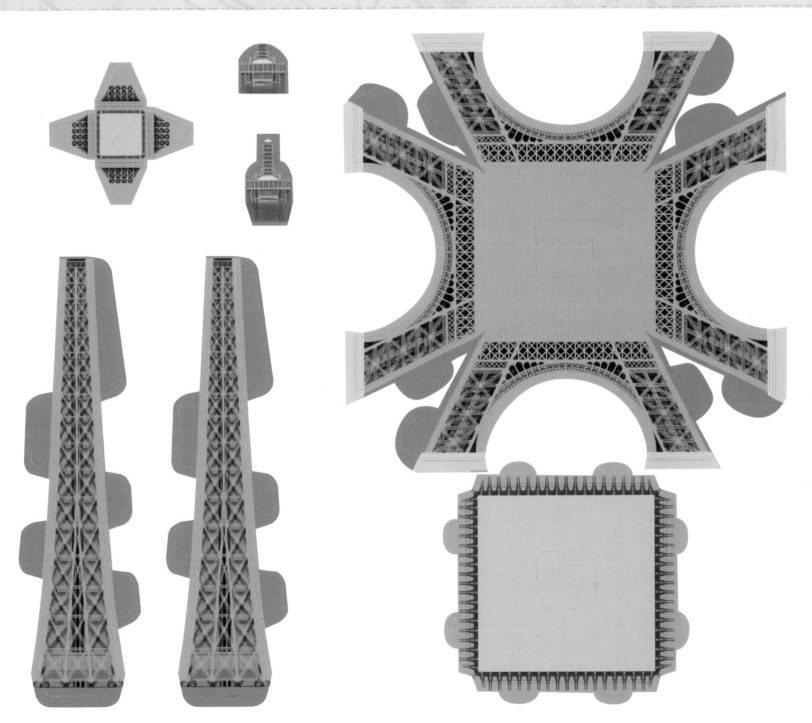

TOWER BRIDGE

London's Tower Bridge is what is called a "bascule" bridge (from the French word for seesaw), and when built it was the largest of its kind in the world. Steam-powered pumps were used to raise the roadway—now electrically driven, although the steam engines are still in place for visitors to see. So sophisticated and effective was the old system that it took only one minute to raise the bascules to their maximum angle of 86 degrees.

The Tower Bridge is one of the most famous symbols of London.

67

TOWER BRIDGE

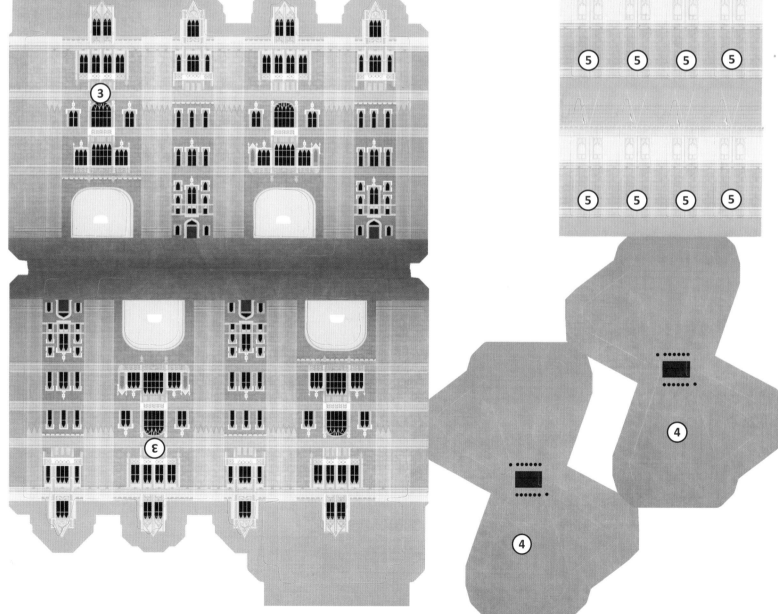

FEATURES:

- *Date of construction* 1886–1894
- *Height* 213 feet (towers)
- *Size* 800 feet (overall length), 200 feet (central span)
- *Commissioner* London County Council
- *Architect* Sir Horace Jones, with Sir John Wolfe Barry
- *Materials* Steel, Cornish granite, and Portland stone
- *Purpose* Bridge and museum

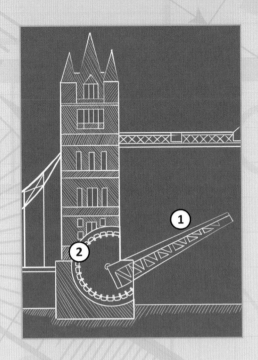

In the original mechanism, bascules (1) were lifted in two stages: energy from two 300-horsepower steam engines (2) was first converted into water pressure, which was then used to raise the bascules. But this would have taken several minutes, holding up the shipping and the traffic for too long.

The answer was the accumulator, a kind of battery that stored hydraulic (water pressure) energy. This was suspended at the top of a tower, then lowered to release enough energy to raise the bascule in under a minute.

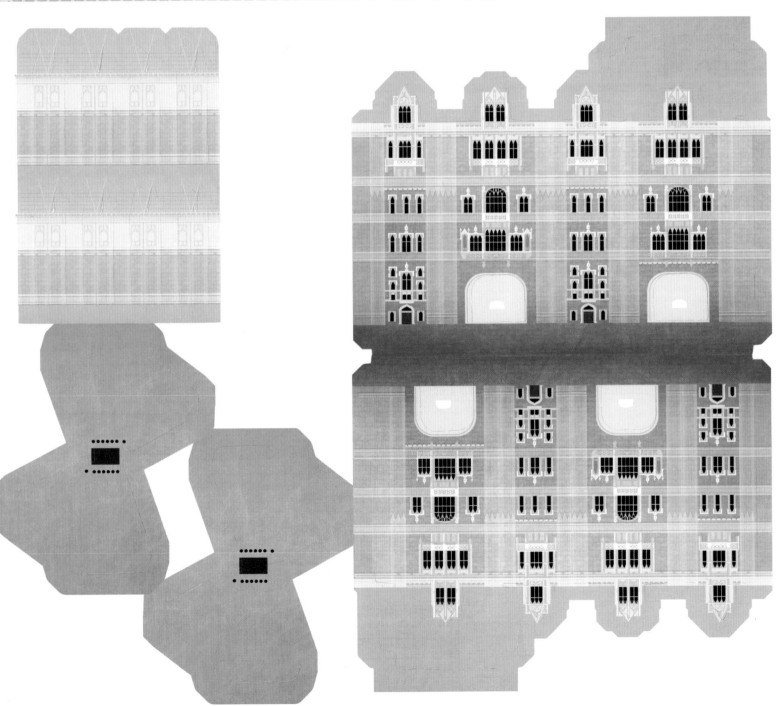

ARCHITECTURAL ELEMENTS

Although the towers give the bridge its fairy-tale profile, they are doing serious work. The two side spans are suspension bridges, so the towers are designed to withstand the forces exerted by the suspended sections. The bridge is supported on two massive piers made of 70,000 tons of concrete. The steel used in the towers and the walkways is clad in stone to add to its fortresslike appearance and to conserve the steel.

◀ *A low-angle view of one of the two towers that support the bridge.*

▶ *The two sections of roadway, or bascules, take just under a minute to be raised.*

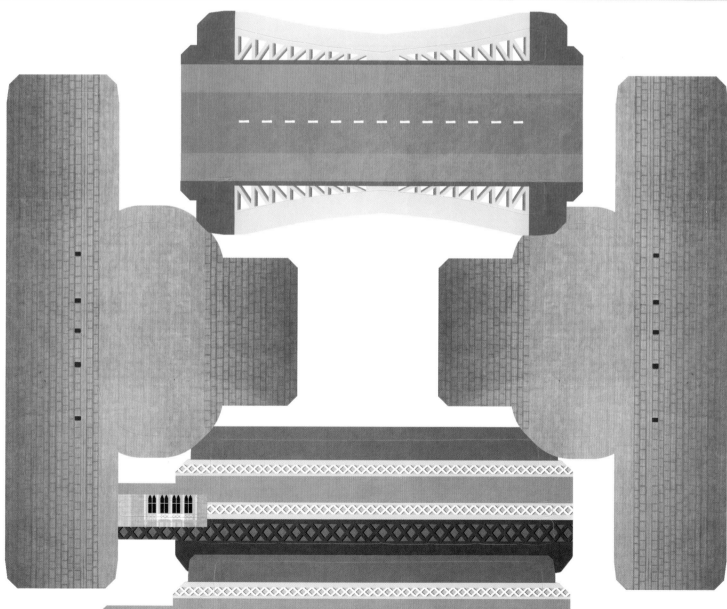

FASCINATING FACTS

• The bridge was designed with high-level walkways, so that the public could still cross when it was in its raised position, but these were closed down in 1910 due to lack of use. They were not reopened until 1982, when the newly covered walkways—part of the Tower Bridge Exhibition—allowed superb views of London and its river.

◄ *The Tower Bridge silhouetted by the morning sun.*

► *The original hydraulic lifting mechanism, now an exhibit in the museum.*

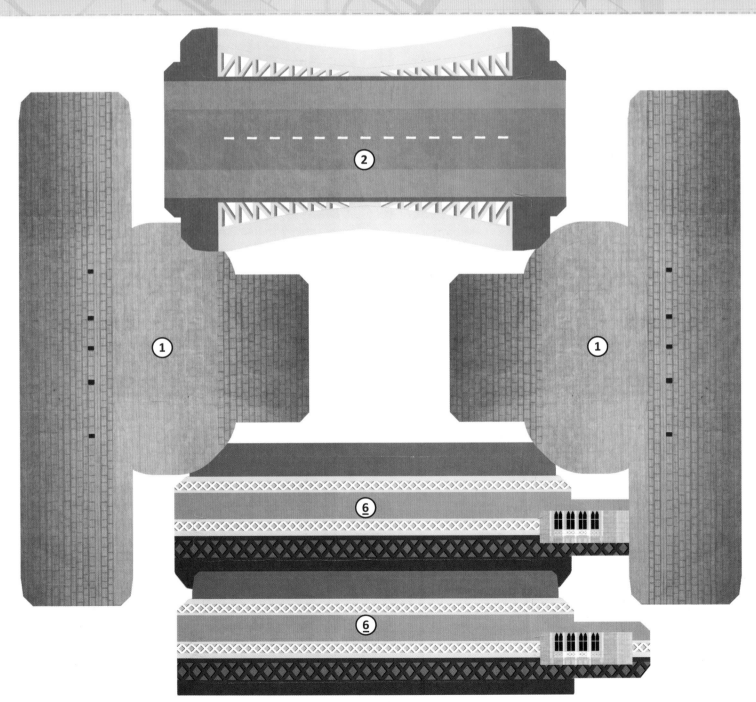

GRAND MOSQUE

The Grand Mosque in Djenné, central Mali, results from local building skills applied on the scale of a French medieval cathedral. What we see today is the third version of the mosque. The first, built in the 13th century, was big enough to house half the city's population; the second was built by the French between 1834 and 1836; the newest, although built during the French colonial period, was designed and constructed by Malian masons.

The Grand Mosque is the biggest mud-built structure in the world.

71

GRAND MOSQUE

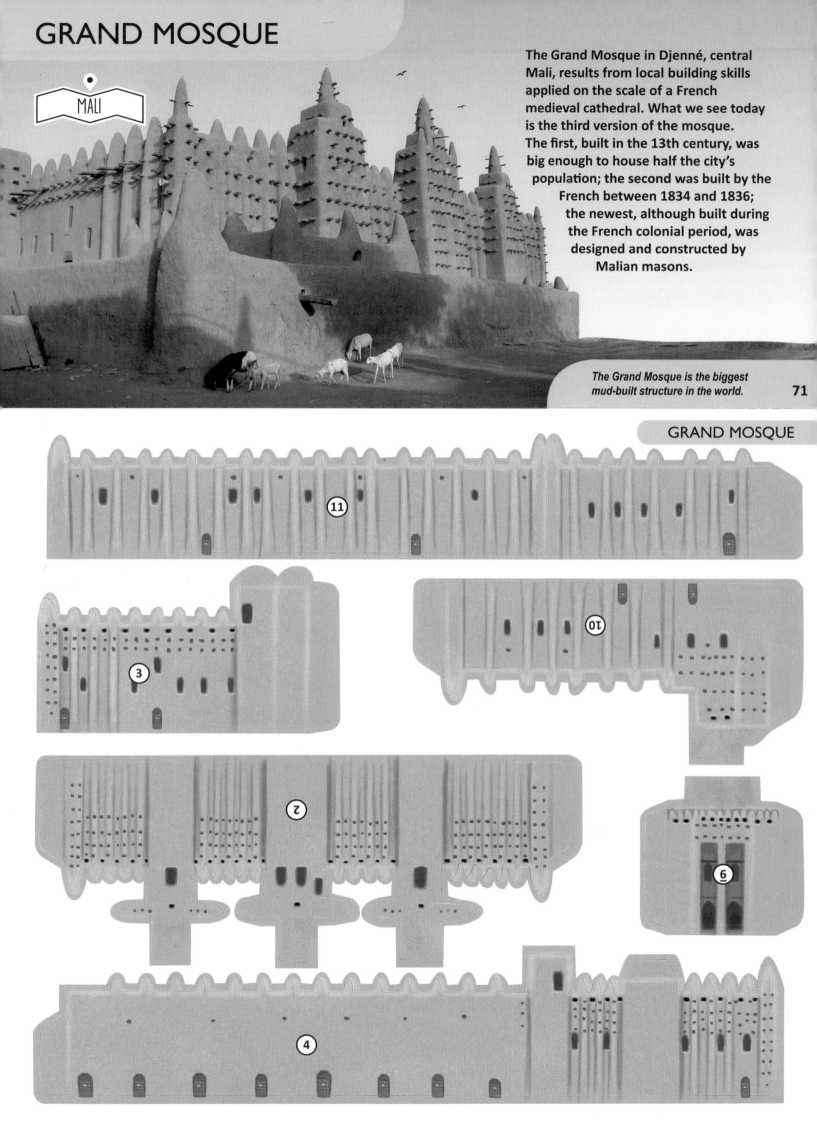

FEATURES:

- *Date of construction* 1892–1907
- *Height* 33 feet
- *Size* 246 x 246 feet (platform), 16–24 inches (thickness of walls)
- *Commissioner* Unkown
- *Architect* Ismaila Traoré of Djenné's Masons' Guild
- *Materials* Mud, sand, rice husks, and palm wood
- *Purpose* Place of Muslim worship

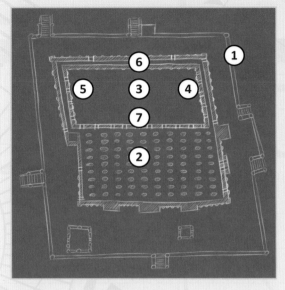

A top view of the mosque shows the entire structure, including the outer walls (1). The roof of the mosque is supported by 90 wooden pillars that span the interior prayer hall (2). Half of the mosque is covered by a roof; the other half is a courtyard, which acts as an open-air prayer hall (3).

A second prayer hall stands in this courtyard and is surrounded by walls to the north (4), south (5), and west (6) and by the mosque itself to the east (7). An arcade encloses the whole courtyard.

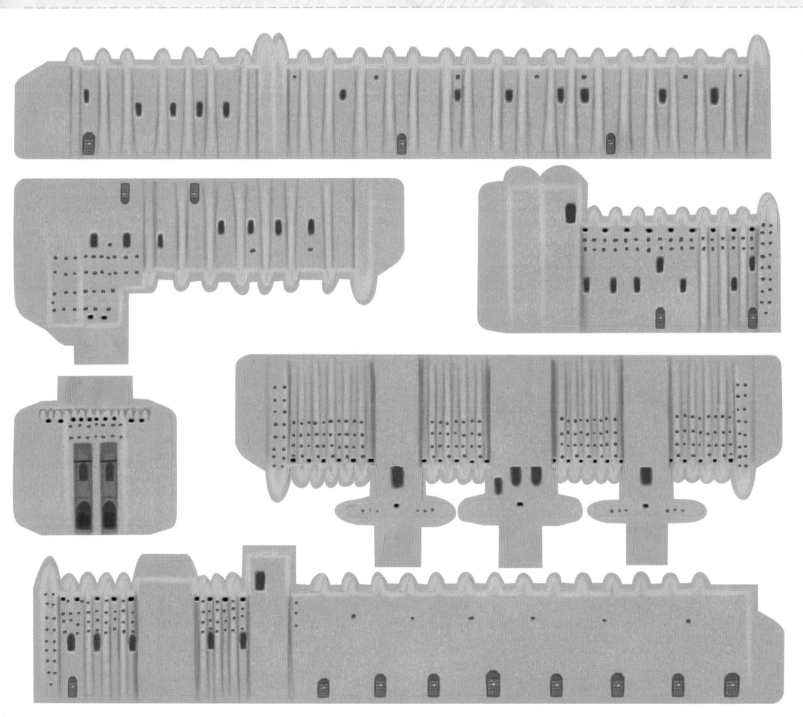

ARCHITECTURAL ELEMENTS

Half the area of the mosque is taken up by an open courtyard; the remainder—the main prayer hall—is covered by a roof supported on 90 wooden pillars. The roof has a number of holes cut out of it, shielded by terra-cotta caps, or cowls, to ventilate the interior. The walls of the surrounding arcade are punctuated by arches. Three minarets feature on the main facade. The structural timbers projecting out allow scaffolding to be attached for maintenance.

▲ The mosque is very much a part of daily Malian life—the market butts up to the mud walls.

◄ The timbers that support the mud walls are left sticking out to attach scaffolding for maintenance.

► One of the minarets with the maintenance supports.

FASCINATING FACTS

• This is truly a community mosque. At the annual festival, Crepissage de la Grand Mosquée (Plastering of the Great Mosque), musicians orchestrate the workers with their drums and flutes, as the local population helps to replaster the mosque's external walls. Women fetch the water and men mix the materials of butter and fine clay, kneading them into a mud plaster and applying to the walls—over time softening the contours of the building.

◄ *The steps leading up to a minaret of the Djenné mud mosque.*

▲ *A Mali stamp bearing the image of the Grand Mosque.*

▶ *The entrance to the mosque.*

74

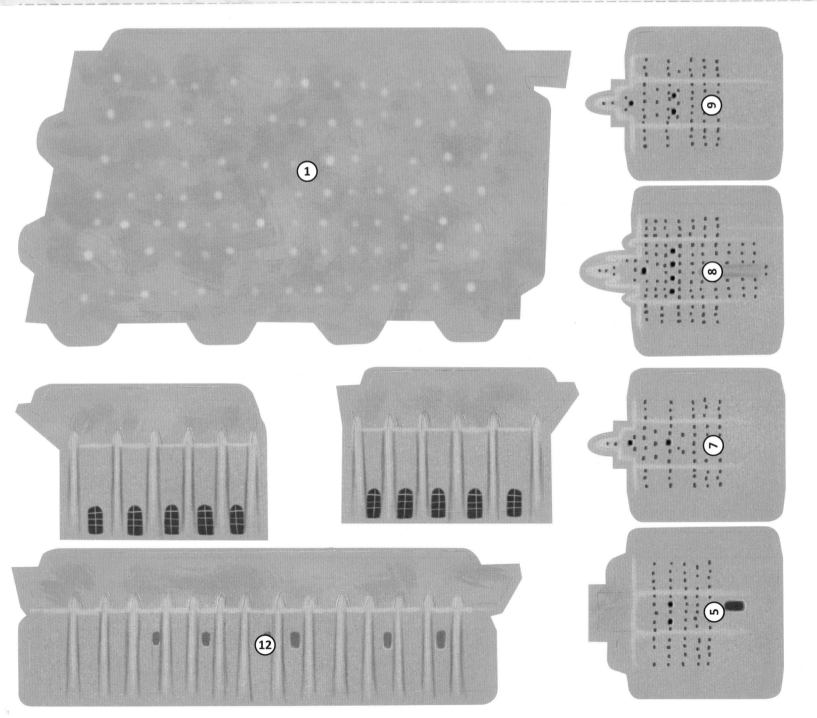

EMPIRE STATE BUILDING

The Empire State Building resulted from a competition between Walter Chrysler of the Chrysler Corporation and John Jakob Raskob of General Motors to discover who could build the bigger building. General Motors won the wager, thanks to the Empire State's added spire, but Chrysler started first and won the time race by 11 months. Even so, because of the competition, the Empire State Building went up at the astonishing rate of 4.5 stories a week and was completed in one year and 45 days.

The Empire State remains the most famous skyscraper in the world.

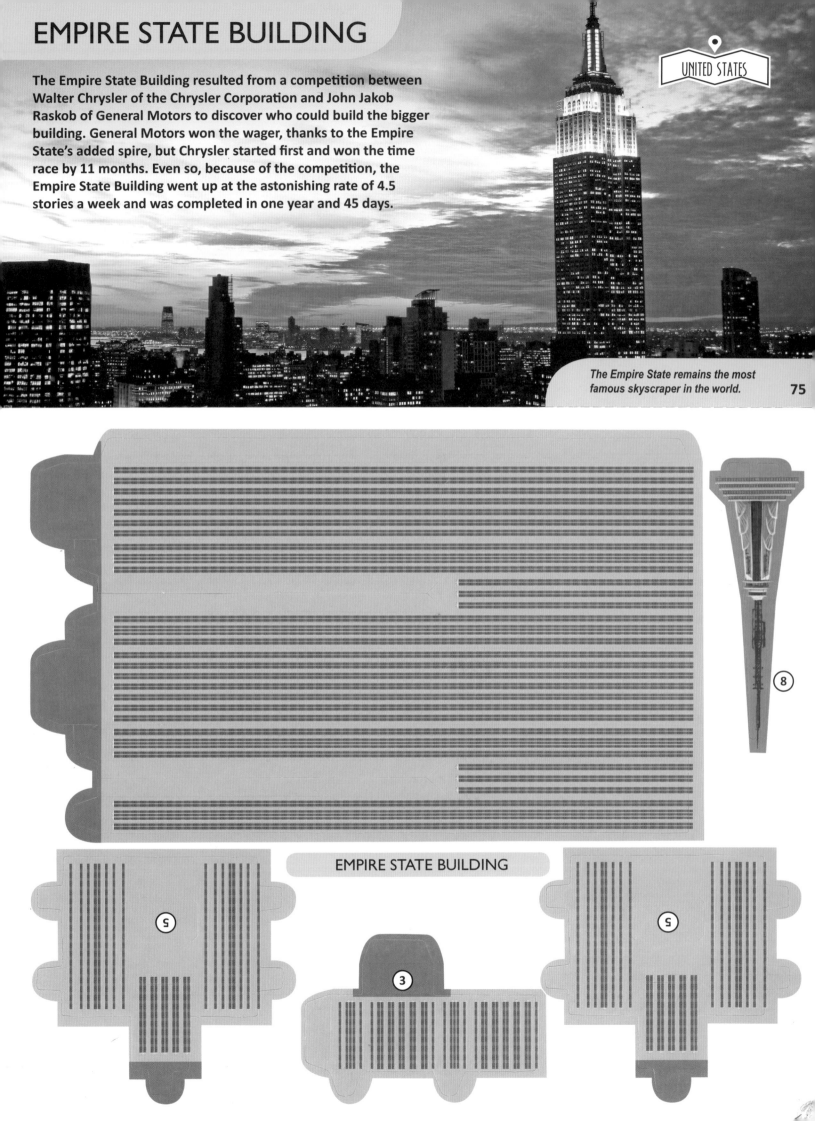

EMPIRE STATE BUILDING

FEATURES:

- *Date of construction* 1930–1931
- *Height* 1,454 feet (base to antenna)
- *Size* 79,288 square feet of floor space over 102 floors
- *Commissioner* John Jakob Raskob
- *Architects* William F. Lamb, and Gregory Johnson of Shreve, Lamb & Harmon Associates
- *Materials* Limestone, granite, brick, and steel
- *Purpose* Commercial offices

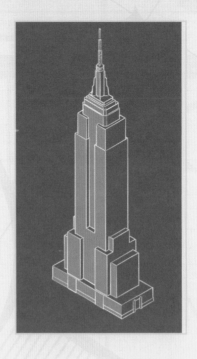

This is what is called an isometric: a drawing that lets us see a two-dimensional object as if it were a three-dimensional object. It allows architects to show the people who commission their buildings what they will really look like. Today this is usually done by means of computer-aided design, or CAD.

Though famous throughout the world, and one of the most beautiful buildings in New York, the Empire State Building is less popular with the people who work there because the steel columns are so tightly spaced that the offices feel somewhat cramped.

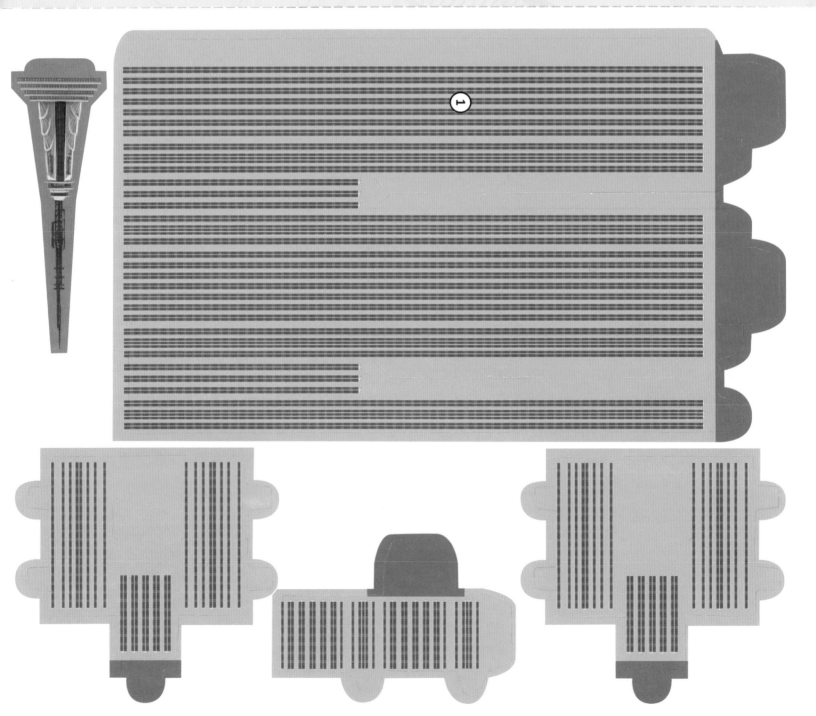

ARCHITECTURAL ELEMENTS

The Empire State Building is typical of the Art Deco style, with its stepped profile reminiscent of an ancient Egyptian or Aztec pyramid. During the 2010 refurbishment, efforts to reduce energy consumption, such as replacing windows, successfully cut more than 38 percent, saving $4.4 million per year. It stands now as a role model for how older buildings can be made more energy-efficient.

▶ *The Empire State still stands proud on the New York skyline.*

▶ *Manhattan—one of the world's great views.*

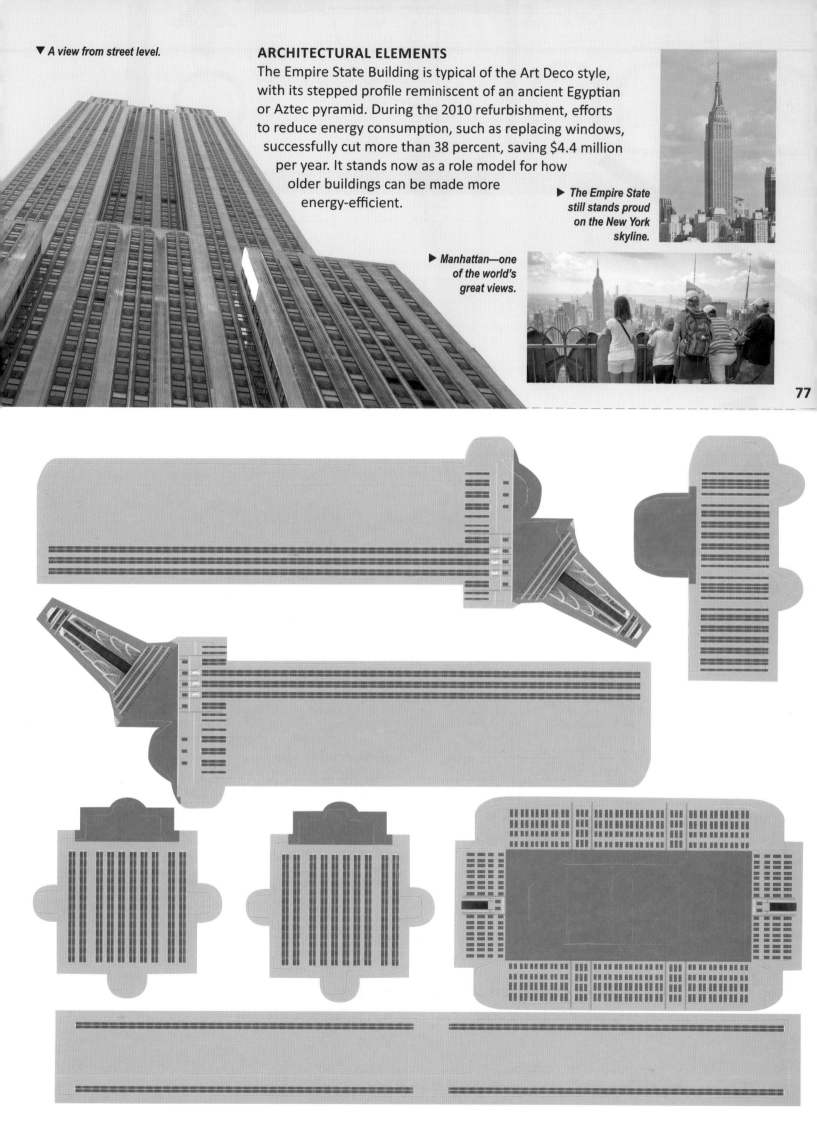

FASCINATING FACTS

• Toward the end of World War II, an Army Air Corps B-25 bomber crashed into the 79th floor of the building in fog. Only two stories were damaged, but 14 people were killed.

• The Empire State gave up its title as New York's tallest building for the second time to the World Trade Center the moment the new One World Trade Center was completed in 2012.

◀ *A classic black-and-white image of a construction worker on the steel frame.*

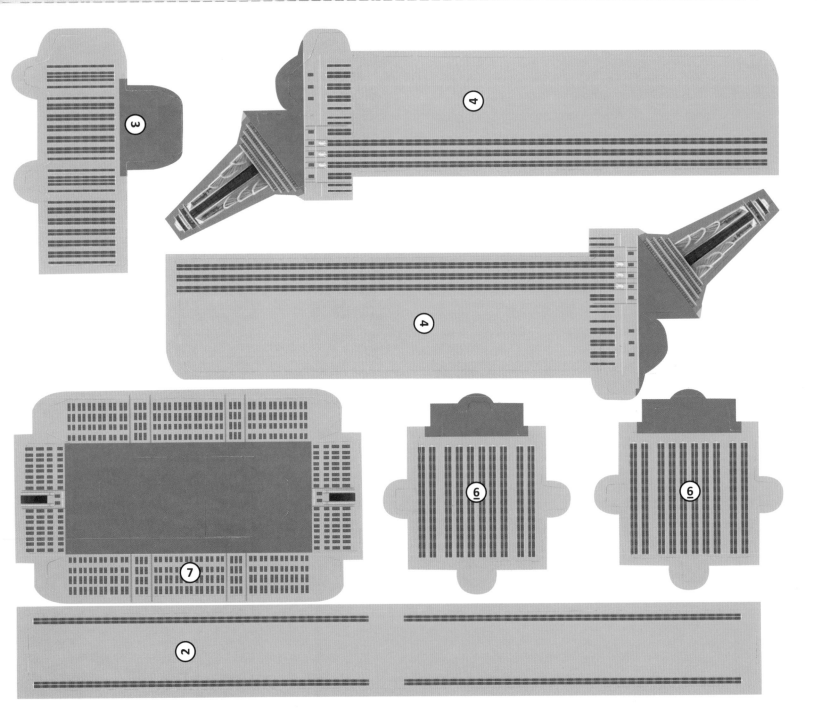

CHRIST THE REDEEMER

The Redeemer, the largest Art Deco statue in the world, stands on top of Corcovado Mountain, in the Tijuca National Forest overlooking Rio de Janeiro. Its massive dimensions make it visible from practically anywhere in the city.

The statue was first proposed in the 1850s by Pedro Maria Boss, a Catholic priest. In 1921 the Catholic Circle of Rio revived the idea. They appealed successfully for public donations to build a statue to "represent the religious strength in the country."

The Redeemer has come to symbolize Rio de Janeiro and Brazil.

79

CHRIST THE REDEEMER

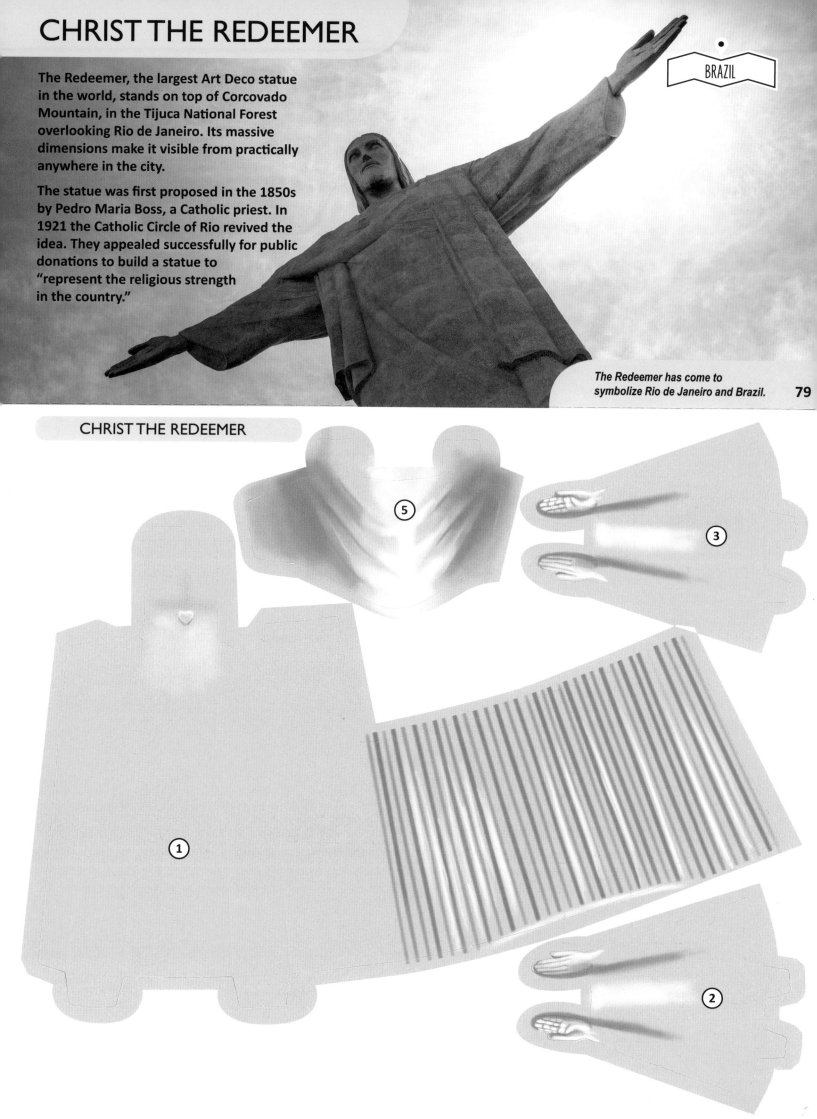

FEATURES:

- *Date of construction* 1922–1931
- *Height* 125 feet (including pedestal)
- *Size* 92 feet (width of outstretched arms)
- *Commissioner* Catholic Circle of Rio
- *Architect* Paul Landowski, sculptor, with engineers Heitor da Silva Costa and Albert Caquot
- *Materials* Reinforced concrete
- *Purpose* Monument and symbol of the city of Rio de Janeiro

A cross section of the giant statue Christ the Redeemer, revealing the iron structure and reinforced concrete underneath the skin of mortar and the mosaic of soapstone tiles. During the major renovation of 2010, the mortar and tiles were removed and cleaned and the cracks in the concrete repaired. A house painter also took the opportunity to repaint one arm and the head in bright colors before giving himself up to the police.

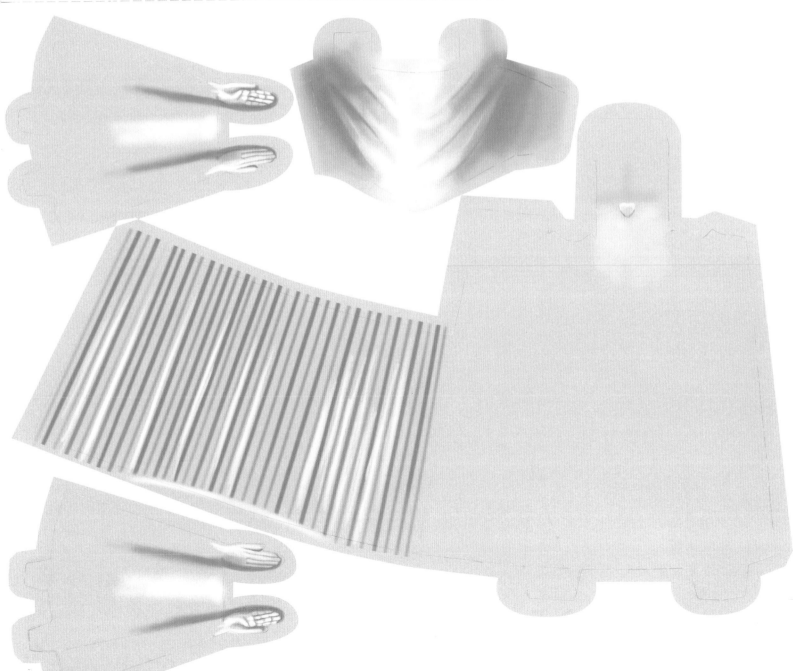

ARCHITECTURAL ELEMENTS

The reinforced concrete construction combined architecture, engineering, and sculpture. With its remote and high position, strong winds, the huge span of the arms, and the odd angle of tilt of the head, the project presented innumerable engineering challenges. It was something of a miracle that there were no fatal accidents during the execution of this Herculean project.

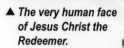
▲ The very human face of Jesus Christ the Redeemer.

◄ The giant statue dominates the city of Rio de Janeiro.

▲ A close-up of the welcoming hand of Christ.

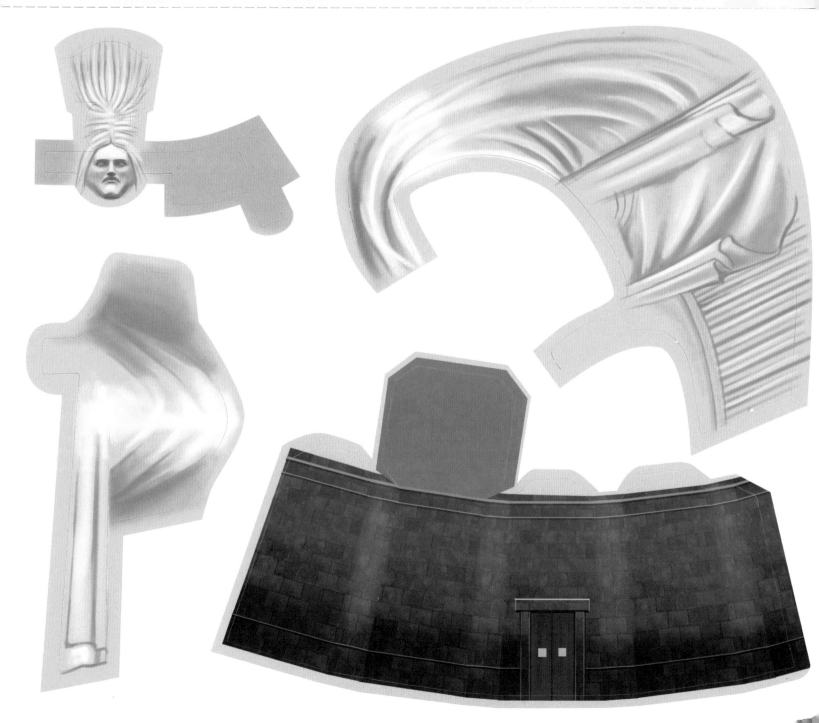

FASCINATING FACTS

• It was the original intention that at the opening ceremony on October 12, 1931, the illumination of the statue would be done remotely from the Italian city of Naples, where the Italian scientist Guglielmo Marconi would transmit an electrical signal to an antenna in Rio de Janeiro. Sadly, bad weather meant the lights had to be turned on locally.

• Weather struck again, in the form of lightning in 2008, causing damage to the fingers, head, and eyebrows.

▶ *An aerial view of the statue on its mountaintop setting.*

82

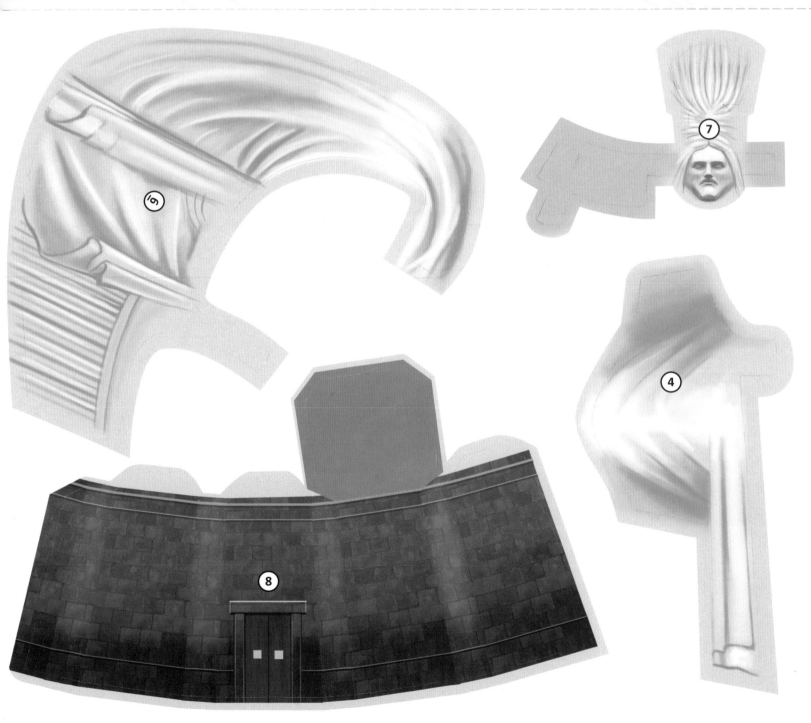

SYDNEY HARBOUR BRIDGE

AUSTRALIA

The bridge across Sydney Harbour was first proposed in 1815 by architect Francis Greenaway, but it was a century before work started. Known locally as simply "the bridge," it was designed and built by the British firm Dorman Long, which had previously built Hell Gate Bridge in New York City and the Tyne Bridge in Newcastle-upon-Tyne. Eighty percent of the steel came from England, and the rest from Australia. To counter concerns about a British contractor, all the labor had to be Australian.

The bridge is nicknamed "the Coathanger" because of its arch-based design.

83

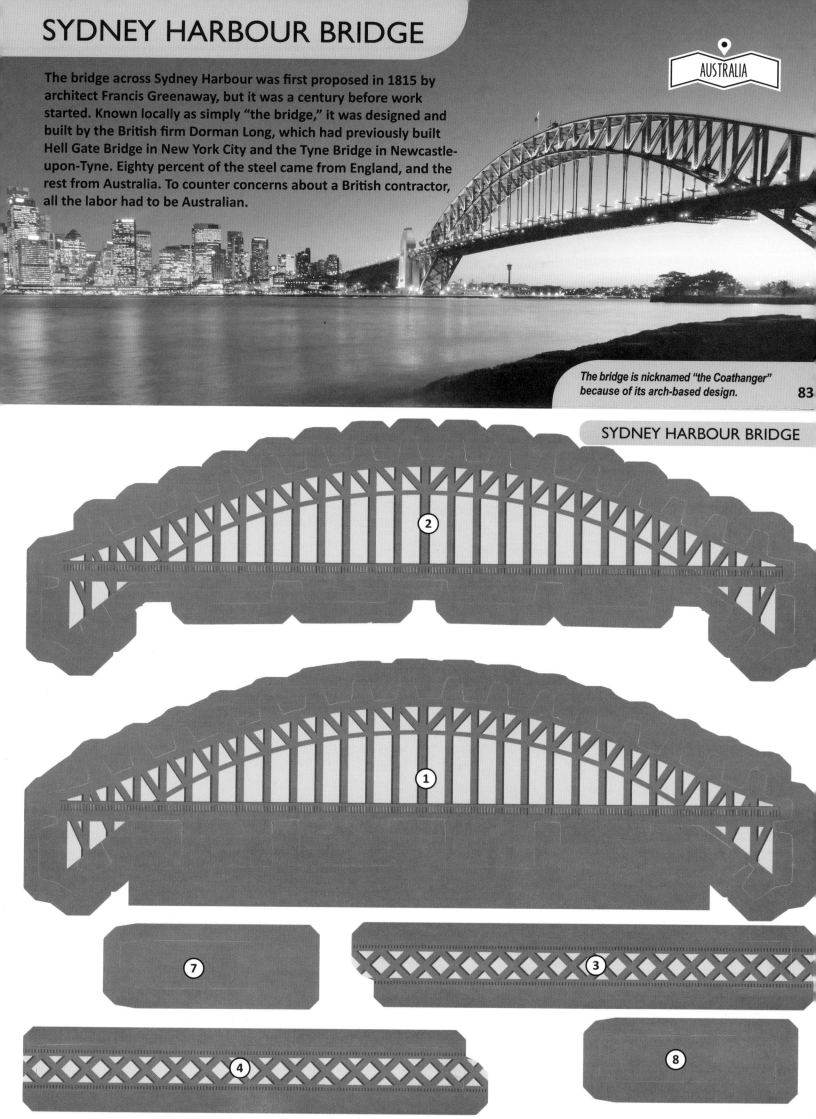

FEATURES:

- *Date of construction* 1924–1932
- *Height* 443 feet (water to highest point of arch)
- *Size* 1,650 feet (main span), 160 feet (width)
- *Commissioner* Dr. J. J. C. Bradfield (Chief Engineer of Sydney Harbour Bridge and Metropolitan Railway Construction)
- *Architects* Dorman Long (designers and builders), Thomas S. Tait (architect), John Burnet and Partners (pylons)
- *Materials* Concrete and gray granite
- *Purpose* Bridge

Below is a cross section of the Sydney Harbour Bridge, showing the riverbed (1), the position of the foundation piles (2), and the anchoring tunnels, as well as the pylons (3), and the superstructure above ground level (4). All drawing was done by hand on cartridge paper or tracing linen with pen or pencil. The copies needed by engineers and builders to do their jobs were usually made by the "blueprint" method, which produced a print of a drawing as white lines on a blue background.

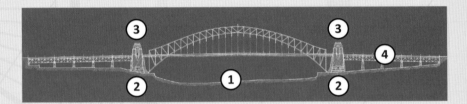

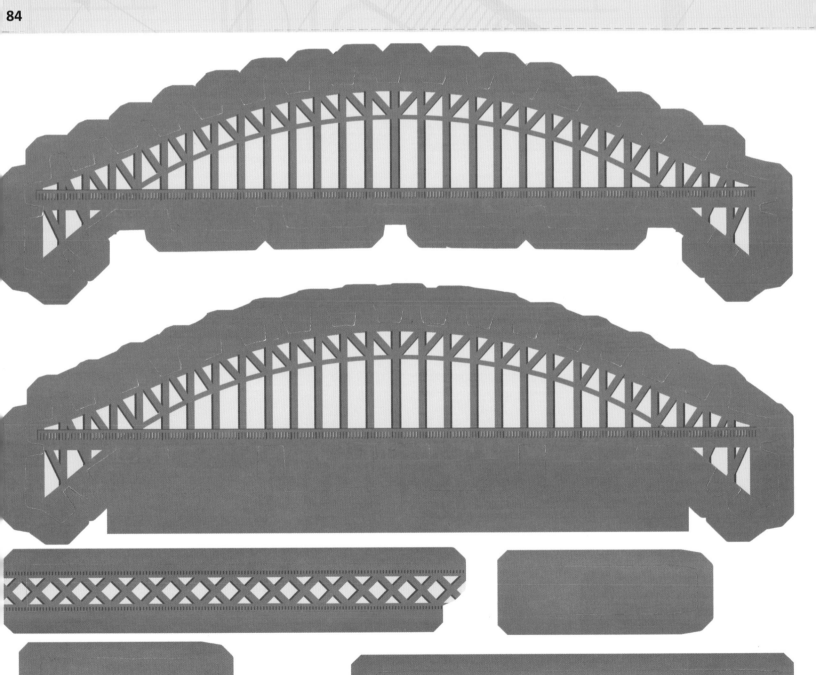

ARCHITECTURAL ELEMENTS

When it opened in 1932, the Sydney Harbour Bridge was the world's longest single-span steel-arch bridge, with a main span of 1,650 feet. Its foundations go down 39 feet, and are set in sandstone. Anchoring tunnels, 118 feet long, are dug into the bedrock at each end. The pylons are made of concrete clad in gray granite from Moruya, on the south coast of New South Wales.

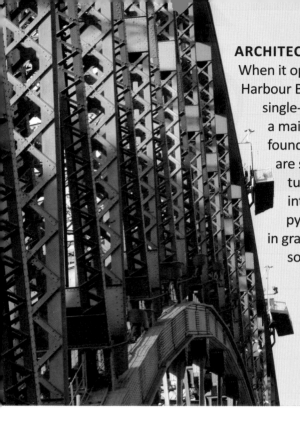

◀ *Close-up of the steel structure of the Sydney Harbour Bridge.*

▶ *The curve of the approach to the bridge makes the crossing much more dramatic.*

▼ *There are six million rivets holding the bridge together, and they were all made in Australia.*

85

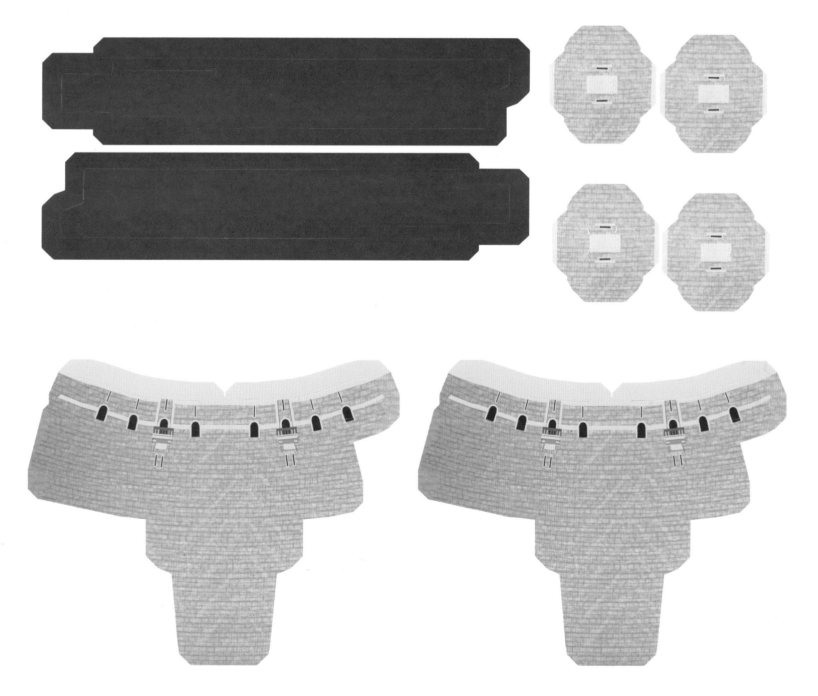

FASCINATING FACTS

• The four 300-foot pylons that mark the "corners" of the bridge are doing little to support it. They are there for aesthetic reasons, and to allay public concerns about the reliability of the bridge.

• Prior to opening, engineers tested the bridge's load-bearing capacity by parking buses, trams, and 96 steam locomotives end-to-end on the roadway. It is just as packed during every rush hour today!

▶*The New Year's Eve firework displays are famous across the world.*

▲ *The deck carries eight lanes of road traffic, two rail tracks, a bicycle path, and a footpath.*

86

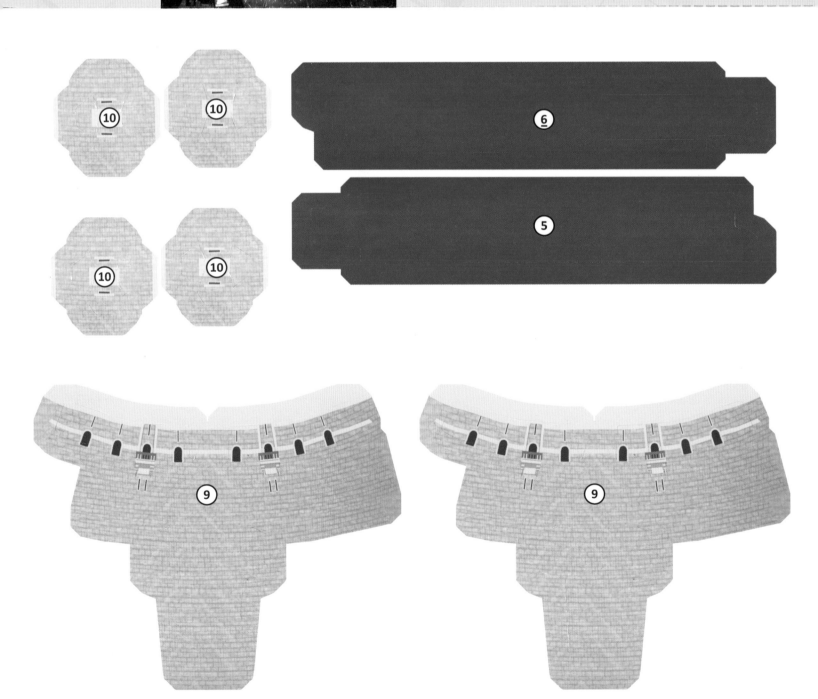

GOLDEN GATE BRIDGE

UNITED STATES

The original proposal, put forward by Cincinnati-born bridge engineer Joseph Strauss, was for a somewhat inelegant suspension-cum-cantilever bridge. This was refined into a pure cantilever structure—its weight carried by tower-supported cables anchored into the bank at either end—by engineer Charles Alton Ellis, and developed into the now-famous structure by the architects, husband-and-wife team Irving and Gertrude Morrow.

The bridge links the city of San Francisco to Marin County.

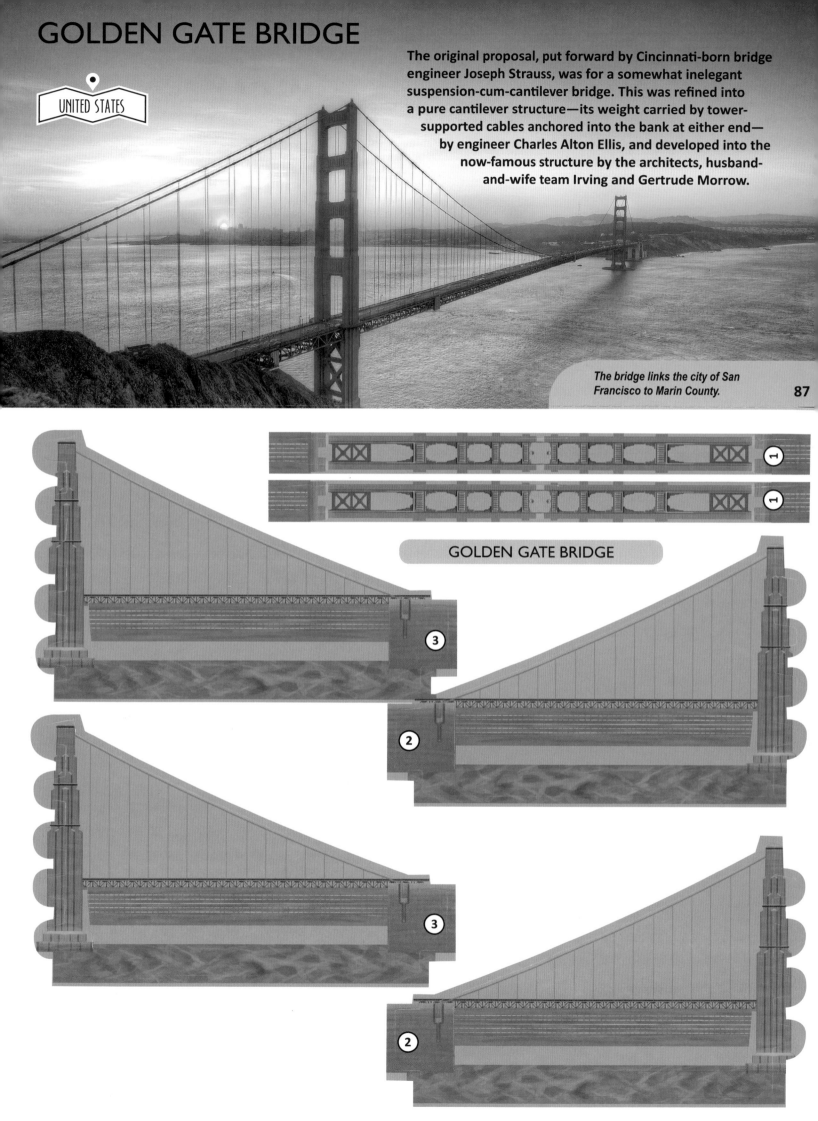

GOLDEN GATE BRIDGE

FEATURES:

- *Date of construction* 1933–1937
- *Height* 746 feet (towers), 220 feet (deck above water)
- *Size* 4,200 feet long, with 80,000 miles of steel cable
- *Commissioner* Joseph Strauss
- *Architects* Irving and Gertrude Morrow, with engineers Charles Alton Ellis and Leon S. Moisseiff
- *Material* Steel
- *Purpose* Bridge

San Francisco is close to the San Andreas fault, where two of the plates that form the surface of the earth meet. Much of the city was destroyed in the earthquake and subsequent fire of 1906. This engineering drawing of the Golden Gate Bridge was done as part of an earthquake analysis to determine the amount of energy the dampers would have to absorb if there was another major earthquake. Work has been going on since 1989 to strengthen the bridge after the study concluded that a quake of similar strength—measuring 8 on the Richter scale of earthquake severity—might very well cause its collapse.

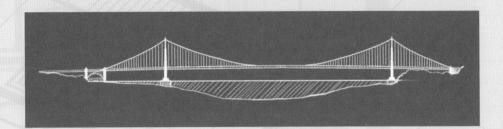

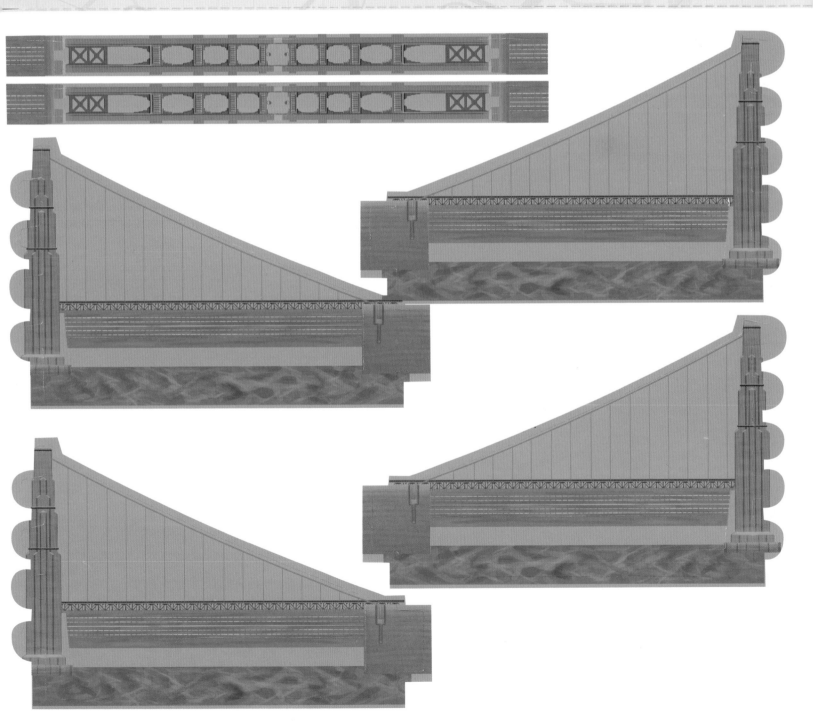

ARCHITECTURAL ELEMENTS

Consultant engineer Moisseiff was keen to put into practice the deflection theory, first put forward by the Austrian academic Josef Melan, who suggested that, as bridge spans become longer and the suspended structure heavier, so the road deck should become lighter and more flexible. It worked here, but was less successful when Moisseiff applied it again at the Tacoma Narrows Bridge in Washington, which collapsed in a storm soon after it opened—and on camera.

◄ *A view along the deck—the International Orange color was originally meant only to be a sealant.*

▲ *The bridge was named one of the seven wonders of the modern world in 1994.*

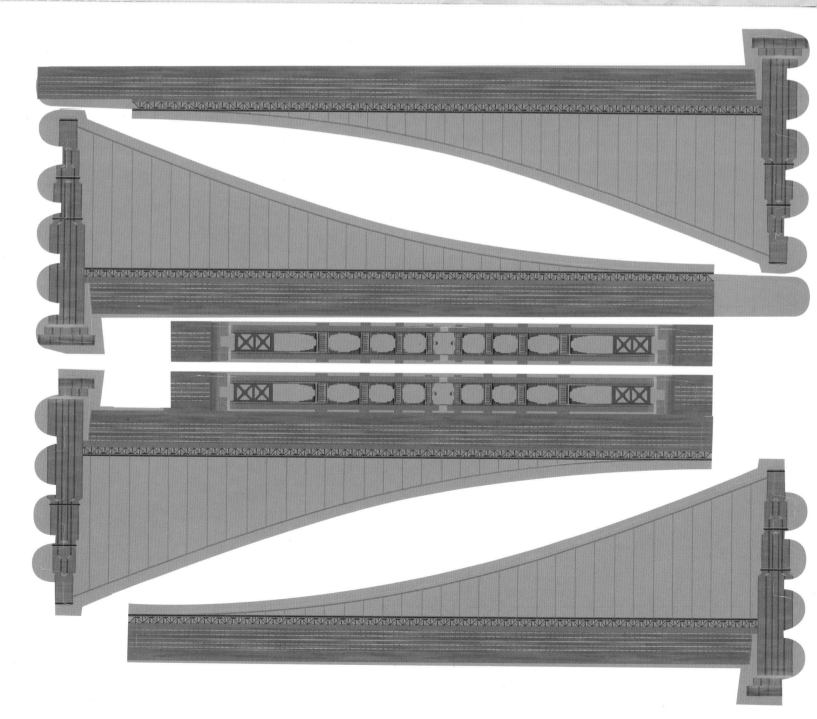

FASCINATING FACTS

• Plenty of structures have been built through public subscription, but only the Golden Gate Bridge has been financed by local residents putting up their homes and businesses as collateral against a $35 million bond taken out by the local authorities.

• Built during the Great Depression over troubled waters (the strait of San Francisco Bay experiences high winds and strong currents), the bridge cost the lives of 11 workers.

◀ *The Golden Gate under construction in 1934. Bridges change the way places relate to one another.*

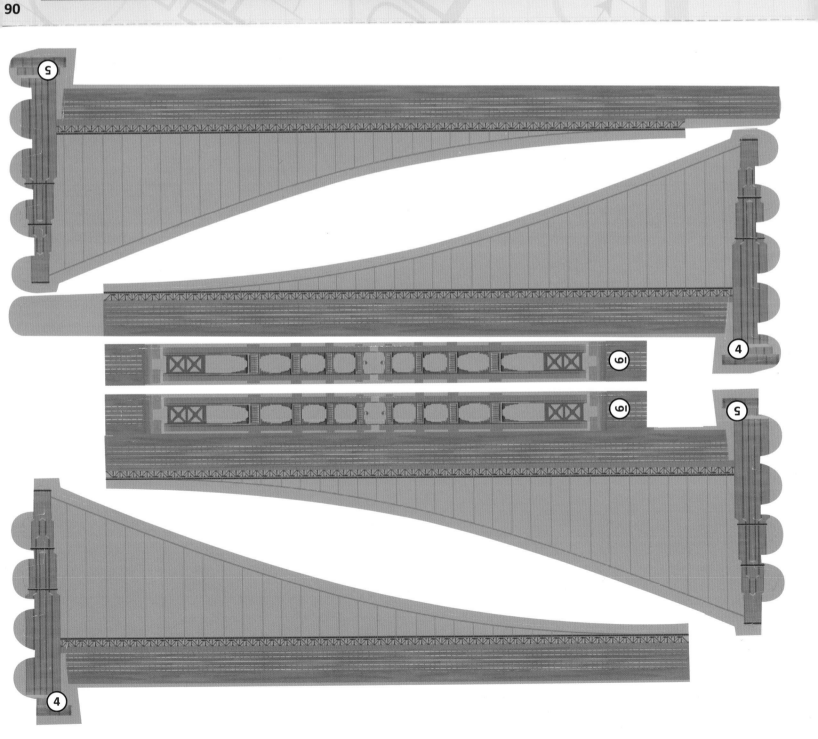

SYDNEY OPERA HOUSE

The relatively unknown Danish architect Jørn Utzon won the competition to design the opera house when the late-arriving jury chair, Eero Saarinen, plucked his entry from those already rejected by the other jurors. Utzon's design was little more than a concept with "geometrically undefined" curves. It took one of the foremost architectural structural engineers of the time, Ove Arup, to determine that the sail roof could be built.

The Sydney Opera House is a center for opera, theater, music, and dance.

91

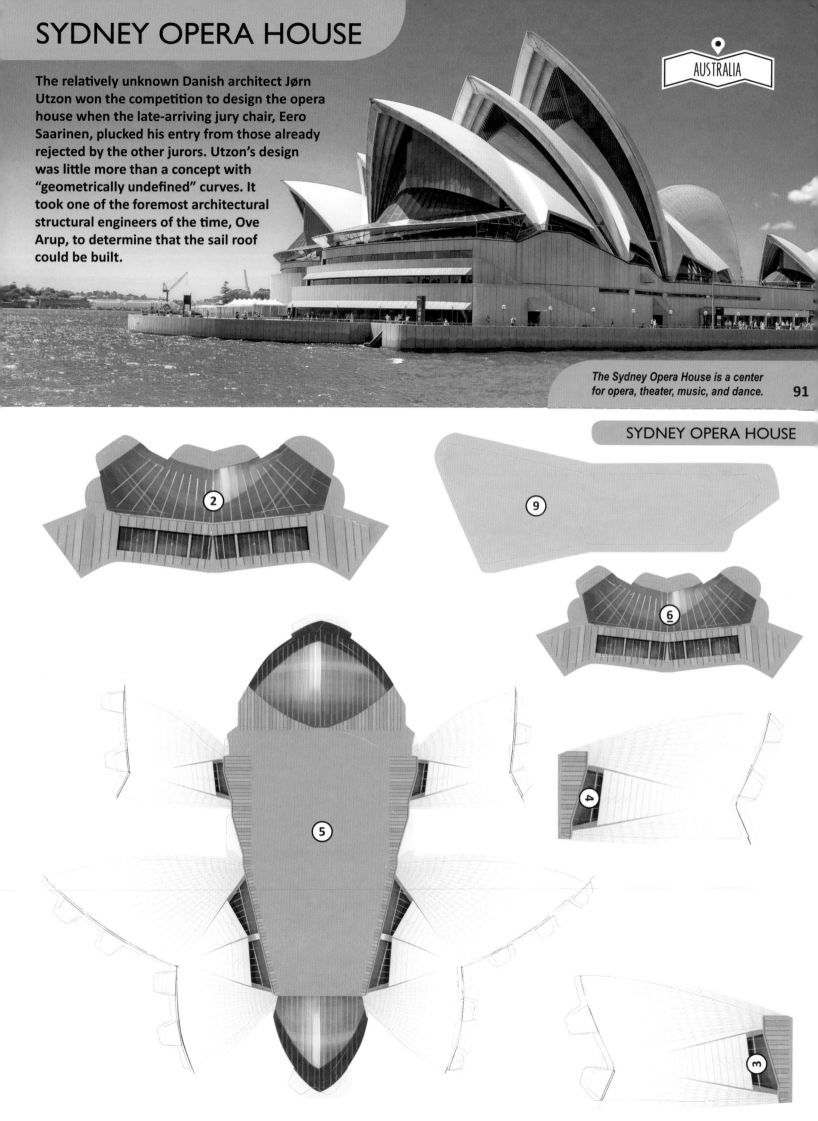

SYDNEY OPERA HOUSE

FEATURES:

- *Date of construction* 1959–1973
- *Height* 213 feet
- *Size* 600 x 394 feet
- *Commissioner* New South Wales government
- *Architect* Jørn Utzon
- *Materials* Concrete; cream and white tiles on the roof structures
- *Purpose* Opera, concert, and theater venues
- *Capacity* 5,738 (all six halls)

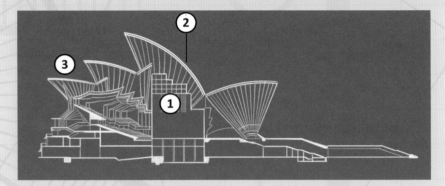

Cross section showing the shells of the roof and the layout of the interiors of the concert halls. The Concert Hall, home of the Sydney Symphony Orchestra, has 2,679 seats (1), and the smaller Joan Sutherland Theatre to the east (2: behind the Concert Hall in this cross section) has 1,507 seats, and is home to Opera Australia and the Australian Ballet. The scale of the shells reflects the headroom needed for the two halls. Smaller shells cover the restaurant spaces (3).

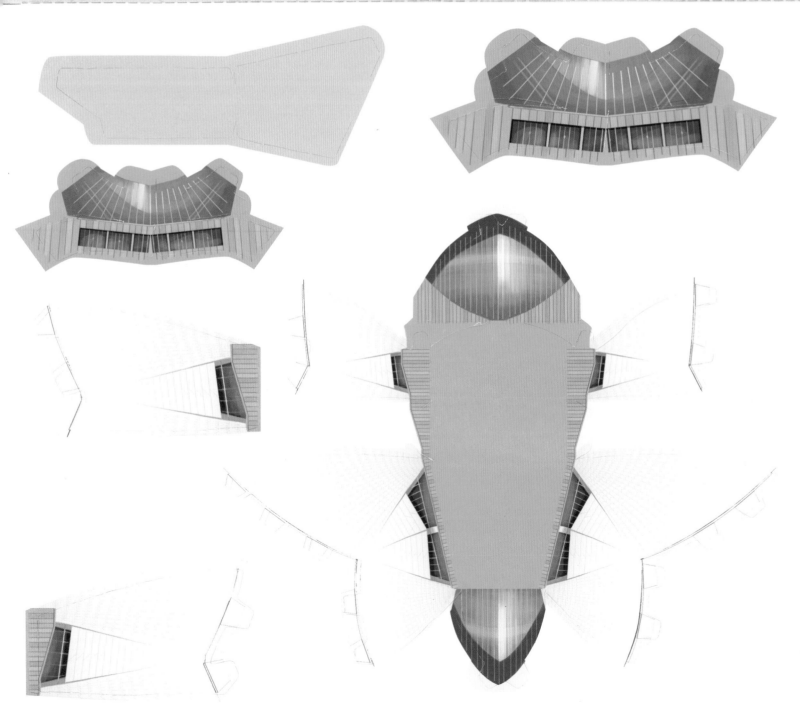

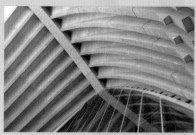

▲ The concrete structural ribs of the shells fan out from the base.

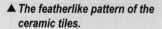

▲ The featherlike pattern of the ceramic tiles.

ARCHITECTURAL ELEMENTS

Working with Arup, Utzon made changes to his original concept to develop a design based on the complex sections of a sphere. The concrete shells that make up the roof are supported by precast concrete ribs. In declaring it a World Heritage Site in 2007, UNESCO stated: "It stands by itself as one of the indisputable masterpieces of human creativity, not only in the 20th century but in the history of humankind."

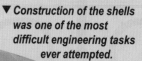

▼ Construction of the shells was one of the most difficult engineering tasks ever attempted.

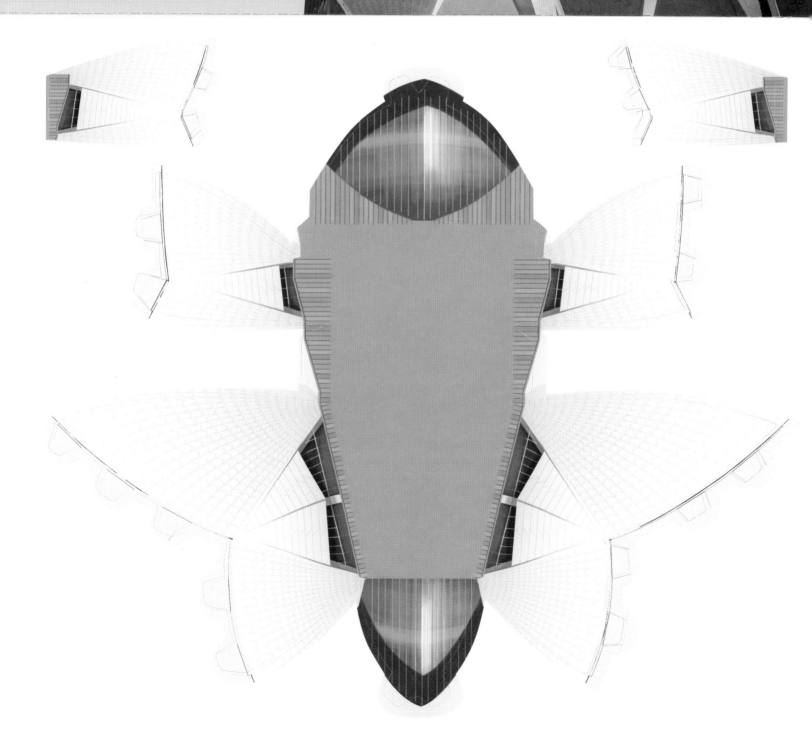

The open ends of the shells are glazed so the light floods inside the opera house.

FASCINATING FACTS

• Utzon did not get to complete the interiors. A change of government in New South Wales meant a new minister of works, who questioned not only the architect's costs and schedules, but even his designs. Utzon was fired and never returned to Australia to see his masterpiece.

• The great American architect Louis Kahn said of the Sydney Opera House: "The sun did not know how beautiful its light was, until it was reflected off this building."

▶ At night the shells glow like ceramic table lamps.

▲ The building resembles a flotilla of yachts.

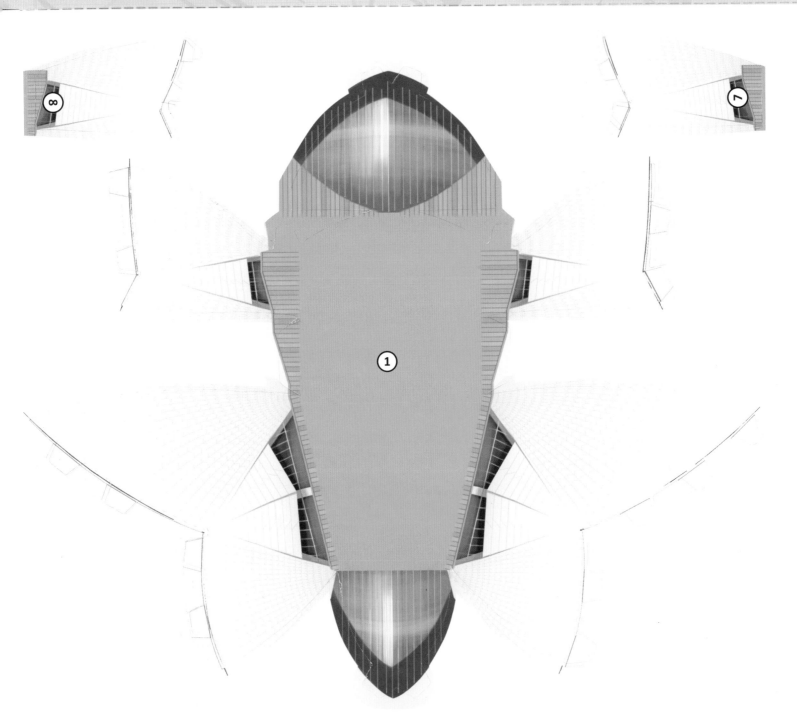

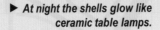

CN TOWER

CANADA

The CN Tower in Toronto opened in 1976 as the world's tallest freestanding structure, reaching more than a third of a mile into the sky. It follows in a tradition of such architect-designed telecom towers in London and Berlin—the BT Tower and Television Tower, respectively. It has since been outstripped by both the Tokyo Sky Tree in Japan (2,080 feet) and the Canton Tower in China (1,969 feet).

The CN Tower is now the world's third-tallest freestanding structure.

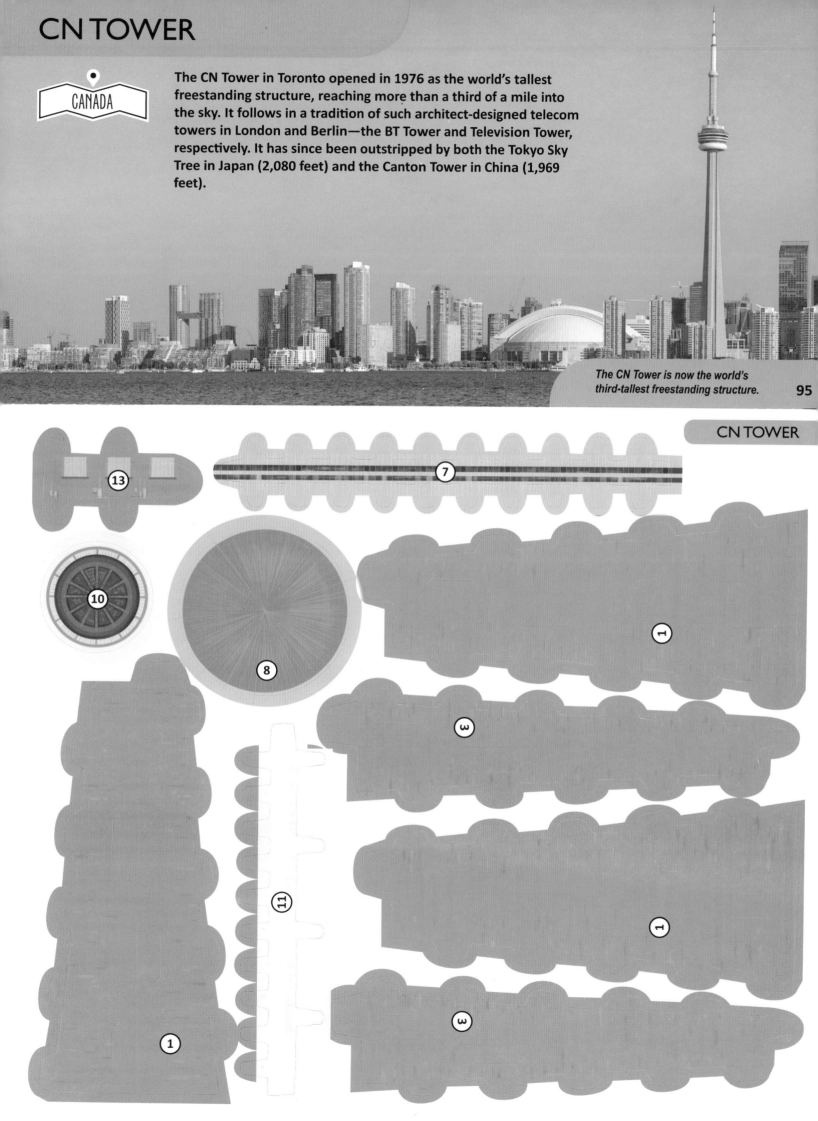

FEATURES:

- *Date of construction* 1973–1975
- *Height* 1,815 feet
- *Commissioner* Canadian National Railways
- *Architect* John Andrews, WZMH Architects
- *Materials* Concrete and steel
- *Purpose* Communications, visitor attraction, and revolving restaurant

Elevation drawing of the tower showing its tapering profile, which, together with a self-supporting hexagonal core, adds stability and strength.

The base has a unique Y-shaped foundation (1) that responds to the condition of the bedrock and supports the three legs of the tower.

A seven-story building called the Skypod, at 1,151 feet (2), houses the revolving restaurant and observation decks.

The Space Deck (3) is a viewing platform 1,465 feet up the tower.

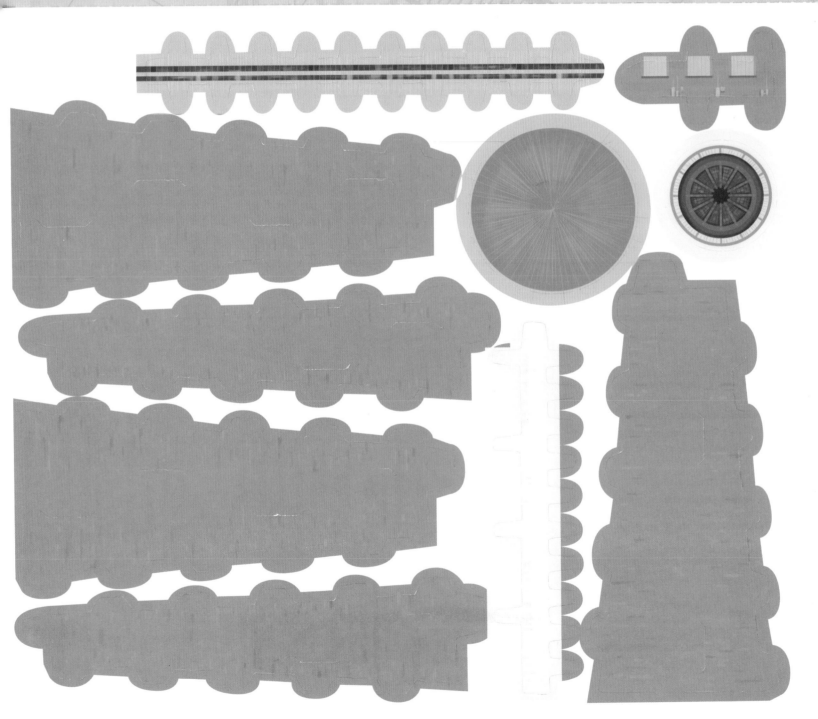

ARCHITECTURAL ELEMENTS

The tower is supported by a Y-shaped base, with each vertical element tapering to merge into an elegant hexagonal core. It comprises 1.4 million cubic feet of concrete, 4,960 tons of reinforcing steel, and 606 tons of structural steel. All the services run through the hollow core. The 335-foot antenna that broadcasts TV and radio signals was made in 36 sections and assembled using a helicopter.

◄ *From below, the tower seems too slender to support its own weight.*

► *The windows light the staircase and its 1,776 stairs.*

FASCINATING FACTS

• The EdgeWalk is the world's highest full-circle hands-free walk—on a 5-foot-wide ledge around the top of the CN Tower's main pod, 1,168 feet in the air. While attached to a safety rail by a trolley and harness system, visitors are invited to lean out backward over the city.

• It takes 72 minutes for the 360-degree restaurant to complete one revolution.

◀ *At night the tower is colorfully lit and becomes a beacon for the city of Toronto.*

▶ *The glass-floored EdgeWalk is not for the fainthearted— 2.5 inches separate you from a 1,122-foot drop.*

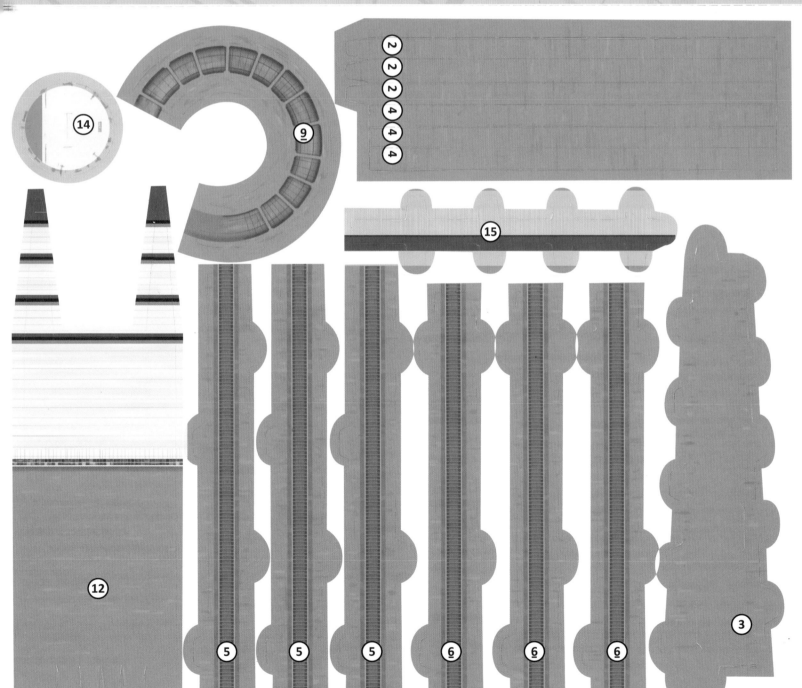

SAGRADA FAMÍLIA

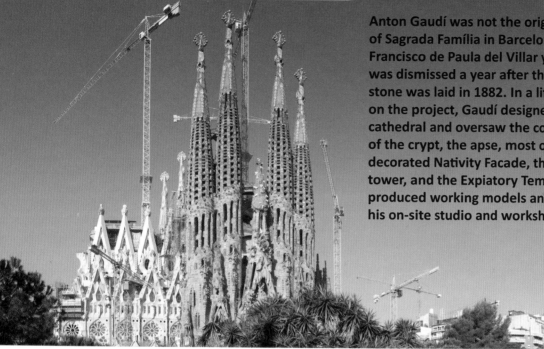

Anton Gaudí was not the original architect of Sagrada Família in Barcelona. That was Francisco de Paula del Villar y Lozano, who was dismissed a year after the foundation stone was laid in 1882. In a lifetime's work on the project, Gaudí designed the entire cathedral and oversaw the construction of the crypt, the apse, most of the highly decorated Nativity Facade, the first bell tower, and the Expiatory Temple. He produced working models and drawings in his on-site studio and workshop.

Gaudí wanted his famous project to be "a cathedral for the poor."

SAGRADA FAMÍLIA

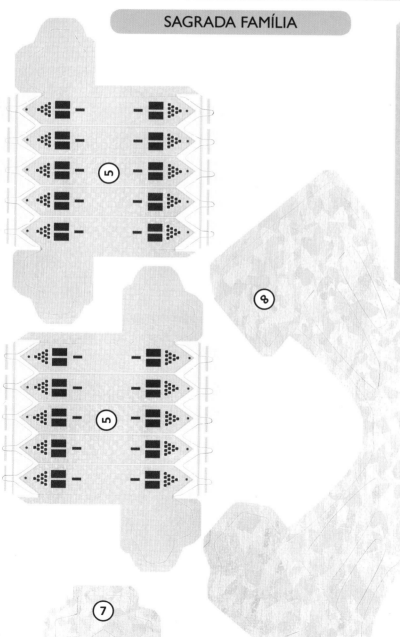

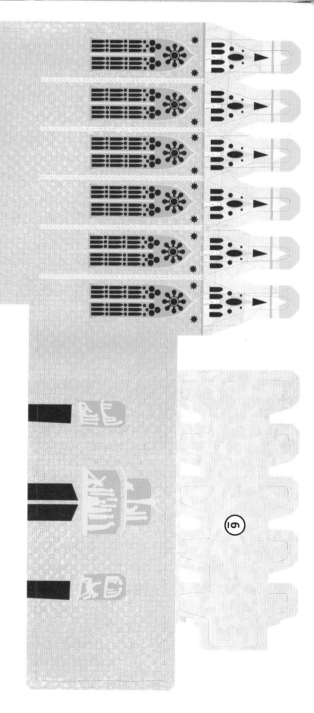

FEATURES:

- *Date of construction* 1882–present
- *Height* 351 feet (Nativity Facade), 558 feet (Jesus Tower)
- *Size* 372 x 265 feet
- *Commissioner* Josep Maria Bocabella i Verdaguer
- *Architect* Anton Gaudí
- *Materials* Porphyry (a hard volcanic rock), basalt, granite, sandstone, and concrete
- *Purpose* Place of Christian worship
- *Cost* Estimated at $1.1 billion

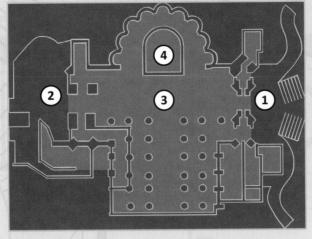

This ground plan of the unfinished cathedral shows the location of the Nativity Facade (1), the Passion Facade (2), and the nave (3). The apse (4), adorned with lizards, serpents, and two gigantic snails, was the first section of the temple to be completed by Gaudí.

The cathedral occupies a complete city block in the Eixample district of Barcelona. But Gaudí's church is a vertical one, designed to be seen from all over the city, with 18 towers all of differing heights; unlike most church builders, he was not concerned with symmetry. All are bell towers, so there are 84 bells in all.

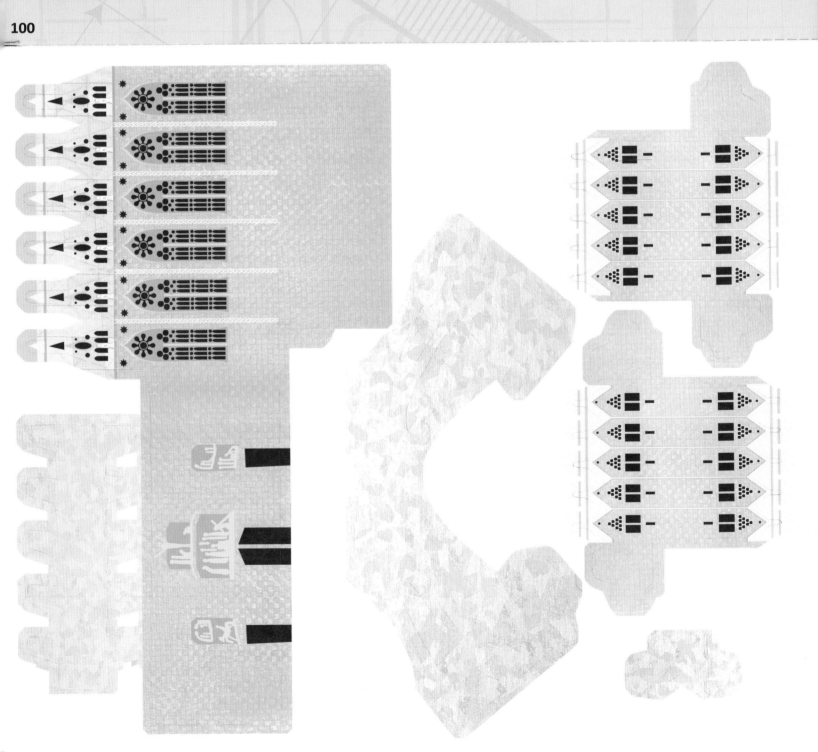

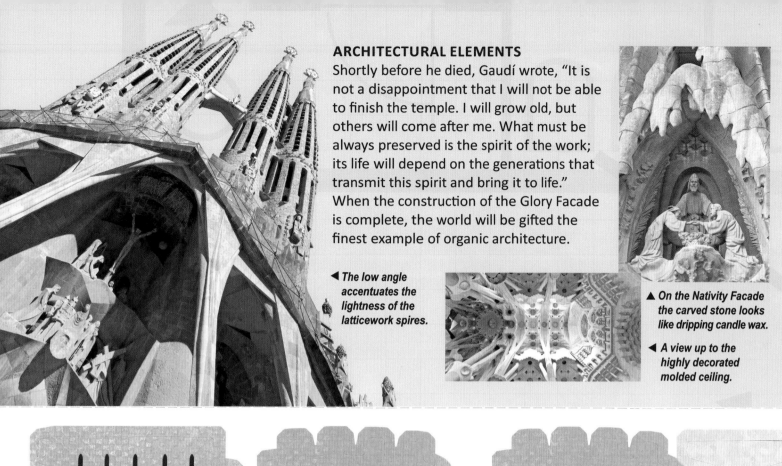

ARCHITECTURAL ELEMENTS

Shortly before he died, Gaudí wrote, "It is not a disappointment that I will not be able to finish the temple. I will grow old, but others will come after me. What must be always preserved is the spirit of the work; its life will depend on the generations that transmit this spirit and bring it to life." When the construction of the Glory Facade is complete, the world will be gifted the finest example of organic architecture.

◄ *The low angle accentuates the lightness of the latticework spires.*

▲ *On the Nativity Facade the carved stone looks like dripping candle wax.*

◄ *A view up to the highly decorated molded ceiling.*

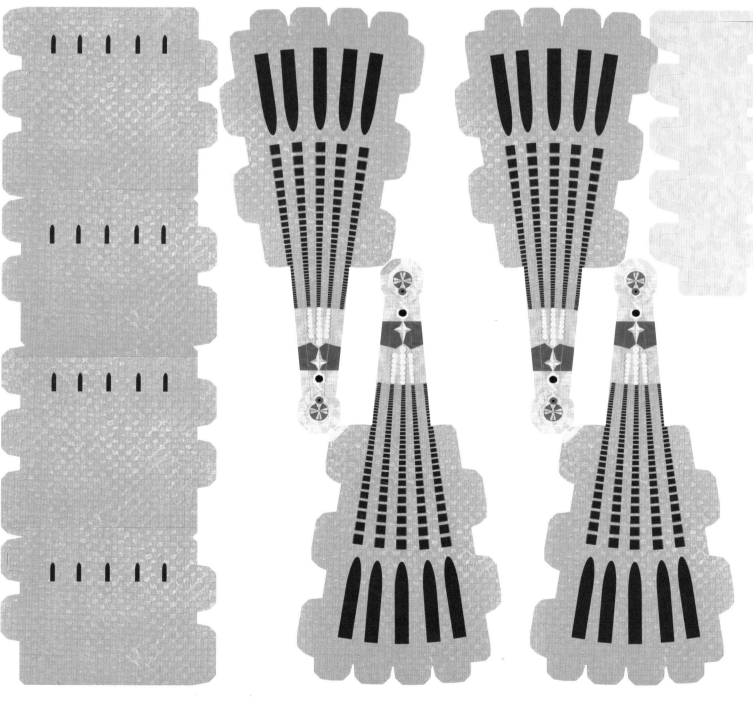

FASCINATING FACTS

• The only one of the 12 towers (one each for the 12 apostles) that Gaudí saw completed was the bell tower on the Nativity Facade, which was finished in 1925. On June 7, 1926, he was knocked down by a tram close to the cathedral and died three days later as a result of injuries. He was buried in the crypt of the Sagrada Família, where his mortal remains rest today.

▲ *A curious view up a snail-like spiral staircase.*

▶ *The spires are topped off with finials—decorative features, many in the shape of flowers.*

▶ *The interior is as full of drama and color as a medieval English cathedral before the Reformation.*

102

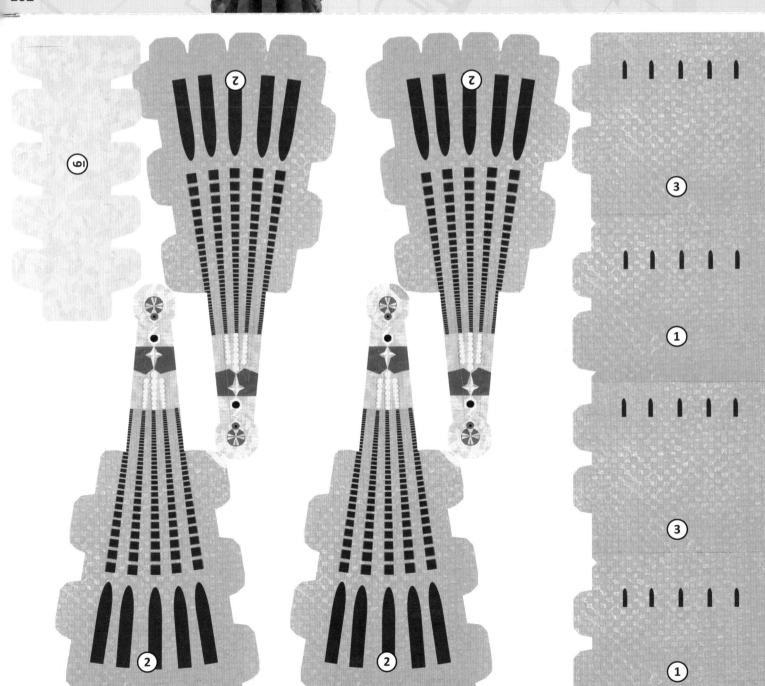

METROPOLITAN CATHEDRAL, BRASÍLIA

Oscar Niemeyer is one of the world's great architects, winner of the Royal Gold Medal and the Pritzker Prize. He was the architect of Brasília, and was still active when he died at 104. The cathedral is one of his masterpieces. The cornerstone was laid in 1958 and its structure was finished in 1960. Its 16 concrete columns represent two hands moving upward to heaven. The cathedral was dedicated in 1970.

FEATURES:

- *Date of construction* 1958–1960
- *Architect* Oscar Niemeyer
- *Materials* Concrete and stained glass

PARTHENON

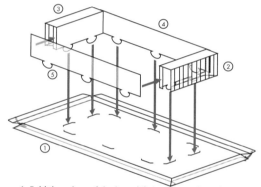

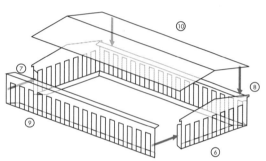

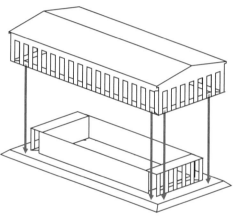

1. Fold the edges of the base (1) down to make a slope and fold the tabs underneath, gluing them together at the corners where they meet. Fold parts 2 and 3 as shown, making sure the front tabs are folded underneath and the side tabs are forward. Stick the sides (4 and 5) to the side tabs on each end. Slot the middle structure into the base as shown, and then stick the front and back tabs to the base.

2. Stick parts 6 and 7 (ends) to part 8 (side) and then add part 9. Fold the top and botttom tabs inward. Fold the roof (10) and stick it to the tabs on the sides—the edge of the roof will slightly hang over the sides.

3. Glue the outer structure to the base. The columns will line up along the edge of the base.

COLOSSEUM

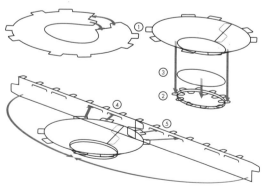

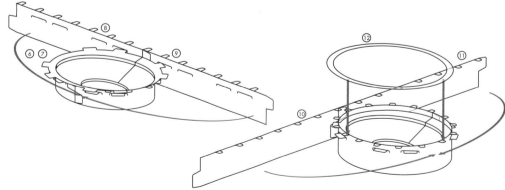

1. Take part 1 and glue the two edges together. This will create an open-ended cone. Take part 2 and glue the ends together to form a ring. Bend the tabs on the top outward and the tabs on the bottom inward. Glue disk 3 onto the tabs at the bottom of the ring. Glue tabs at top of part 2 onto the center of part 1.

2. Glue parts 4 and 5 together. While bending the edges to form a ring, slot the tabs around the edge of part 1 through the slits in 4 and 5.

3. Join parts 6 and 7 together and then join the two ends to form an open cone. Attach it to the top tabs on parts 4 and 5 as shown.

4. Glue parts 8 and 9 together. Bend the two ends around to create a ring as with parts 4 and 5. Slot the tabs in on parts 6 and 7 through the slits as before.

5. Glue parts 10 and 11 together and then bend the ends to make a ring. This will make the outer wall. Stick part 12 to the tops of the outer and inner wall to make the roof.

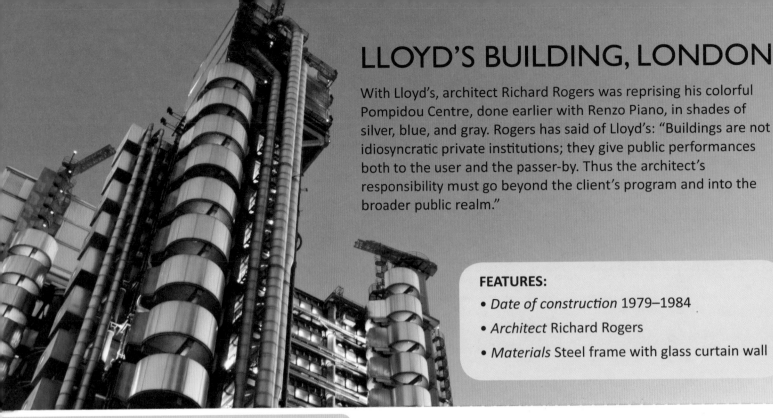

LLOYD'S BUILDING, LONDON

With Lloyd's, architect Richard Rogers was reprising his colorful Pompidou Centre, done earlier with Renzo Piano, in shades of silver, blue, and gray. Rogers has said of Lloyd's: "Buildings are not idiosyncratic private institutions; they give public performances both to the user and the passer-by. Thus the architect's responsibility must go beyond the client's program and into the broader public realm."

FEATURES:
- *Date of construction* 1979–1984
- *Architect* Richard Rogers
- *Materials* Steel frame with glass curtain wall

CHICHEN ITZA

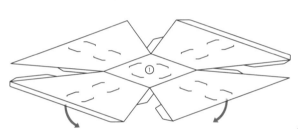

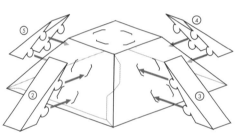

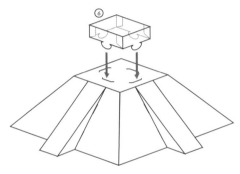

1. Take part 1 and fold the sides down to form a flat-topped pyramid. The tabs on each side edge need to be folded and glued to the inside of its neighboring side. The two tabs on the bottom need to be folded underneath—this helps to keep the sides straight.

2. Assemble the steps: 2, 3, 4, and 5. Fold the sides inward and slot them into the slits in the main section of the pyramid—one step per side.

3. Take part 6, fold the shorter sides down, and fold the tabs inward. Fold the longer sides down and glue them to the tabs. Slot into the top of the pyramid.

ANGKOR WAT

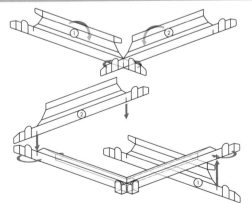

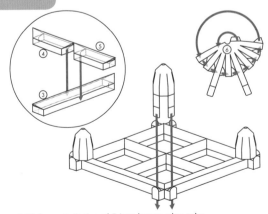

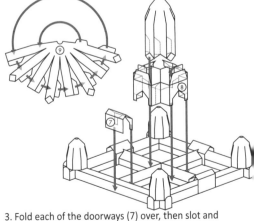

1. Take one set of parts 1 and 2 and slot the ends together as shown. Fold the top parts of both pieces inward toward the center of the model and glue the tabs of part 1 to the inside wall of part 2. Fold the edges where they slot together backward and stick to the side. Slot the other part 1 into the end of the previous piece and then the other part 2. Fold over the ends and stick as before.

2. Make parts 3, 4, and 5 into boxes, glue tabs together and stick them in the middle of the frame as shown. Assemble each of the corner towers (part 6). Glue the tab on the arms to the back of its neighbor. As they stick, they naturally start to form a rounded tower. Rotate the final tabs to meet the starting arm. Slot the long tabs through the base where shown, fold the ends over, and stick together to secure them.

3. Fold each of the doorways (7) over, then slot and glue them on the base as shown. Fold part 8 into a thick cross shape and slot this over the middle of the base. Make the central tower (9) in the same way as the smaller towers. Fold back the tabs on the long arms, add glue to the tabs, and stick them to the roofs on the base. Fold in the roofs on part 8 and stick the tabs to the tower.

GUGGENHEIM, BILBAO, SPAIN

This is perhaps the only building in the world to have a social phenomenon named after it: the "Bilbao effect" describes the regeneration of a city kick-started by a single new building. Frank Gehry was invited by the ailing Basque port to design a new museum. The result was the first architectural to be created in gleaming titanium, and an early example of shapemaking, in which form definitely does not follow function.

FEATURES:

- *Date of construction* 1993–1997
- *Architect* Frank Gehry
- *Materials* Titanium, steel, and limestone

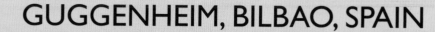

NOTRE-DAME DE PARIS

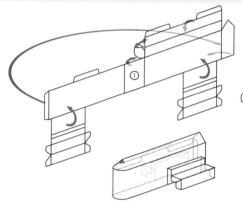

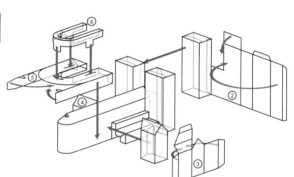

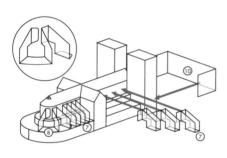

1. Take part 1. Fold the bits hanging down upward and stick to the main wall. Fold the other pieces as shown in the diagram to form big steps. Fold the roof down, roll the long wall around a pencil, and stick the top tabs to the roof edge—this makes a nice round end. Roll around the top of the roof into half a cone and stick the tab.

2. Assemble the front (2) into boxes and stick to the end tabs on the steps on either side of part 1. Assemble parts 3 and 4 and stick them to part 1 and the tabs on the steps as shown. Fold the sides of part 5 down and join the end strip to form a curve. Do the same for part 6. Slot 6 into 5 and then stick both to part 1, and the end tabs to parts 3 and 4.

3. Assemble all the flying buttresses (7). Stick three on top of the big steps as shown. Stick another two next to part 3 and repeat on the other side of the model. Fold part 8 as shown in the circle and then stick it on the end as shown. Do the same on the other side with part 9 at the end. Fold the sides of part 10 and stick them to the sides of the front.

ST. BASIL'S CATHEDRAL

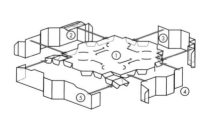

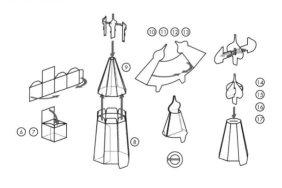

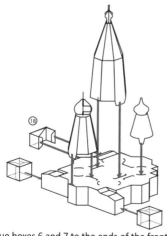

1. Take part 1 and fold down all the glue tabs along the edges. Fold part 2 and attach it to part 1. Match the part number to the tab with the same number, fold the roof over, and stick it to 1. Attach the rest of the sides (3, 4, and 5) in order.

2. Fold parts 6 and 7 into boxes and glue. Roll parts 8 and 9 into flat-sided cones and glue together. Glue the top together and slot it into the roof.

3. Roll parts 10–13 into cones, fold the tower parts into the middle, and glue together.

4. Make parts 14–17 into flat-sided cones. Glue the roofs together and slot each one into their respective towers.

5. Glue boxes 6 and 7 to the ends of the front. Match the numbers to get them in the right place. Slot the center tower (8) into the middle. Slot the four small towers in their slits (10–13). Slot the four middle-sized towers into their slits (14-17); the edge tabs glue behind the sides. Fold part 18 and glue the roof to form a gentle slope. Attach it to the edge.

EDEN PROJECT, CORNWALL

The Eden Project is a showcase for global biodiversity. Built in a Cornish china clay pit, the plastic biomes form the largest plant enclosure in the world, with tropical and temperate regions. The steelwork weighs less than the air contained inside the biomes; the plastic—ETFE—is a hundred times lighter than glass. To ensure maximum daylight to nourish the plants, their positioning was determined by solar modeling.

FEATURES:
- *Date of construction* 1998–2000
- *Architect* Nicholas Grimshaw
- *Materials* ETFE and steel (biomes); glulam (glued laminated) wood and copper (visitor center)

HIMEJI-JO

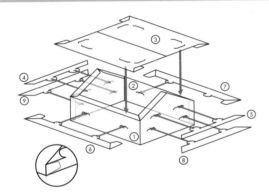

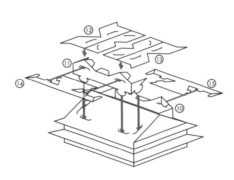

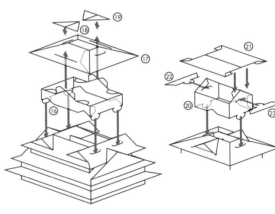

1. Take parts 1 and 2 and stick them together at the edges to form the base. Fold the roof (3) in the middle and stick it to the top tabs on the base. Slot parts 4 and 5 into the sides and stick the edges to the little edge tabs on the roof (see circle). Slot parts 6 and 7 into the slits as shown, and then 8 and 9, sticking them to the tabs on 6 and 7.

2. Fold the edges of parts 10 and 11 and slot them into the roof (3). Fold parts 12 and 13 along their middles and stick them to the tabs on parts 10 and 11. Slot part 14 into the slits in part 11 where shown, then slot the tabs on the angled bit into the slits in the roofs (12 and 13). This will make another sloping roof. Stick the side tabs to the roof as before. Do the same with part 15.

3. Fold up part 16, glue together, and slot it into the roof as shown. Fold part 17 to form a gentle sloped roof, and stick together. Slide the roof over part 16, making sure the front and back goes through the slits. Fold 18 and 19 and attach them to the tabs to form roofs. Assemble parts 20–23 to form the final piece, and slot it into the slits in part 17.

ST. PETER'S BASILICA

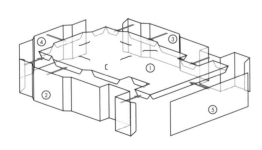

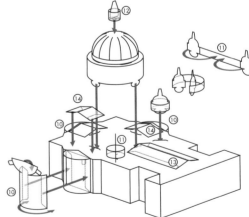

1. Fold down the tabs on the roof (1). Take parts 2, 3, 4, and 5 and stick to the folded-down tabs on the roof.

2. Take the dome (parts 6 and 7). Stick part 6 to one of the "petals" in part 7 as shown. Fold down the next "petal" and glue it to the band. Keep going until the dome is formed.

3. Assemble the dome base with parts 8 and 9. Glue part 9 to 8 on one of the tabs and then roll part 9 into a cylinder, gluing the tabs as you go. Slot the dome into the slits in the top.

4. Fold the side tabs on parts 10 (there are three of them) inward and curl to form a curved wall. Stick one to both sides and back. Curl the roofs down to form a shallow sloped roof and stick the tabs to the inside. Take part 11, fold the edges inward, roll the strip to form a cylinder, and glue the middle pieces together. Do the same with part 12. Fold the roofs (13 and 14) and stick them where shown. Slot everything in place.

MILLAU VIADUCT, FRANCE

The initial design concept by engineer Michel Virlogeux was for a multispan, cable-stay bridge. A subsequent international architecture competition selected Norman Foster's scheme, which was closest to Virlogeux's, making them natural partners. The resulting structure, which often seems to sail above the clouds, is not technically a bridge but a viaduct, because it is supported on piers—of between 246 and 804 feet. Stabilizing masts rise another 285 feet above the road deck.

FEATURES:

- *Date of construction* 1993–2004
- *Architect* Norman Foster, with engineer Michel Virlogeux
- *Materials* Steel and concrete

TAJ MAHAL

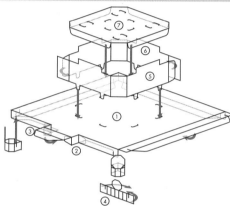

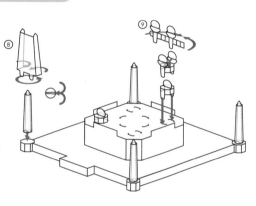

1. Fold the walls of part 1 down and fold the bottom tabs underneath. Stick parts 2 and 3 to the walls as shown. Fold the edges of part 4 around and slot the end tabs into the slits in the corner of part 1. Fold the roof down and stick to part 1. Do the same for each corner. Stick 5 and 6 together to form the walls, stick the roof (7) to the walls, and slot into part 1 where shown.

2. Roll each part 8 into a cylinder. Fold the edge tabs inward and stick together. Stick each one to the roofs of the corners. Fold the side of part 9 into an octagon and stick. Fold the roof on each side down and stick the domes together. Do the same for all four and slot them into part 7 as shown.

3. Take the dome (parts 10 and 11). Stick part 11 to one of the "petals" in part 10 as shown. Fold down the next "petal" and glue it to the selected band. Keep going until the dome is formed. Take part 12 and make it into a shallow cone, sticking the tab to the inside of the edge. Fold the bottom tabs up and stick it to the top of the dome. Slot the dome into the slits as shown.

GREAT WALL OF CHINA

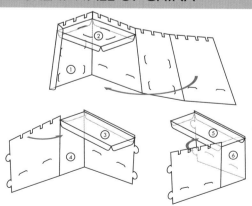

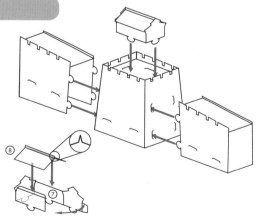

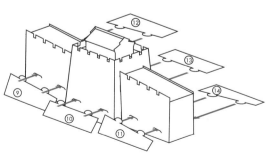

1. Assemble the tower by sticking the tabs on part 2 to the inside of the tower (part 1) as shown. Roll the side around, sticking to part 2 as you go, and glue the wall to the edge tab.

2. Take part 3 and stick it to the tab on the back of part 4. Fold part 3 down and stick it to the side wall as shown. Do the same for the other part of the wall using parts 5 and 6.

3. Fold the sides of part 7 to assemble the hut. Take the roof (8) and fold and glue the center section as shown in the circle, then glue it to the tabs on part 7.

4. Slot the four assembled parts together as shown: hut in the top, parts 3 and 4 in the back, and parts 6 and 7 in the front.

5. Slot the sloping ground sections into the wall as shown.

BMW CENTRAL BUILDING, LEIPZIG

On entering what would otherwise be a bland steel shed the size of 50 soccer fields, the extraordinary power of Zaha Hadid's vision is revealed. Half-finished BMWs glide above your head on elevated conveyor tracks, making their silent, stately way between the body shop and the paint shop, weaving above 500 office and production staff. This gloriously simple idea is the embodiment of Zaha's sinuous, sensuous architecture.

FEATURES:

- *Date of construction* 2001–2005
- *Architect* Zaha Hadid
- *Materials* Steel, concrete, and glass

U.S. CAPITOL BUILDING

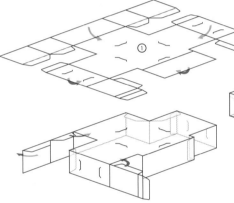

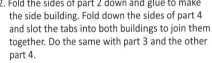

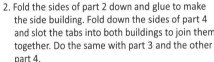

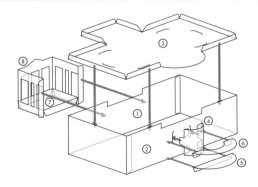

1. Take part 1 and fold the sides down as shown. Fold the side walls inward and stick the tabs to the underside of the roof.

2. Fold the sides of part 2 down and glue to make the side building. Fold down the sides of part 4 and slot the tabs into both buildings to join them together. Do the same with part 3 and the other part 4.

3. Take the dome (parts 5 and 6). Stick part 6 to one of the "petals" in part 5 as shown. Fold down the next "petal" and glue it to the band. Keep going until the dome is formed. Glue part 8 to part 7 on one of the tabs and then roll part 8 into a cylinder, gluing the tabs as you go. Slot the dome into the slits in the top. Fold the edge tabs of part 9. Roll the edge to form a cylinder and stick the tabs to each other in the center. Stick to the top of the dome.

THE WHITE HOUSE

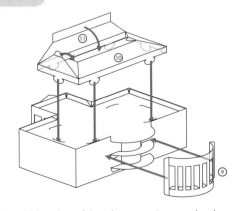

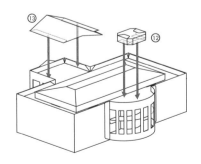

1. Glue parts 1 and 2 together along the edges. Fold the tabs on the roof, part 3, upward and stick them to the inside of the sides—the edges of the tabs will line up with the top edges of the sides. Take part 4 and fold the top and bottom tabs inward and slot the middle tabs through the slits in part 2. Stick part 5 under part 4 and line up part 6 with the artwork, then stick on the side. Take part 7, fold the tabs down and stick to the bottom of part 8. Stick parts 7 and 8 onto parts 1 and 3.

2. Fold the edges of the tabs on part 9 outward and stick it on the side—this creates a nice curve. Join parts 10 and 11 together. Fold down the long roof on part 10 and stick the tabs on both the end roofs to the flat part of 10. Fold down the long roof on part 11 and stick the flat part on top of the other flat part.

3. Fold all the tabs on part 12. Stick the top tabs to the underside of the roof and then stick the whole piece to the roof where shown.

4. Fold the tabs underneath on part 13 and then fold it in the middle of the roof. Stick the tabs to the roof where shown.

SCOTTISH PARLIAMENT, EDINBURGH

The Scottish parliament was designed by the Catalan architect Enric Miralles, who died during the construction. It was completed by his wife Benedetta Tagliabue. It forms an organic transition between Edinburgh's Old Town and the Scottish countryside. The interiors, especially the cryptlike entrance hall and the eccentrically dramatic chamber, are equally impressive. One of the statements on an outer wall reads: "Say little and say it well." This building says a lot, but still says it well.

FEATURES:
- *Date of construction* 2005
- *Architects* Enric Miralles and Benedetta Tagliabue
- *Materials* Granite, steel, concrete, oak, and glass

HOUSES OF PARLIAMENT

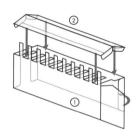

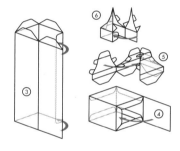

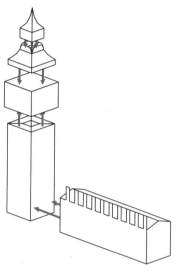

1. Take part 1 and fold the sides down as shown. Assemble the roof (part 2). Fold the long side tabs underneath and stick them to the top of part 1 over the long holes. Fold the end tabs down and then fold the end of part 1 and glue it to the side and roof tabs at the same time.

2. Fold the tower (part 3) into a square tube. Make a box from part 4—fold the top down and the bottom up, and then glue the sides to the tabs as shown.
3. Assemble parts 5 and 6 in the same way. Fold the tabs on the sloping roofs and stick them to the inside of the next slope. Do each section in turn.

4. Assemble the tower by gluing the tabs and sticking the parts together as shown.

NEUSCHWANSTEIN CASTLE

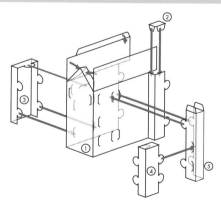

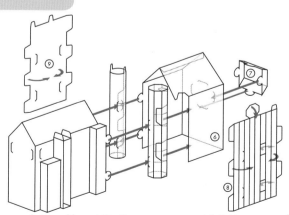

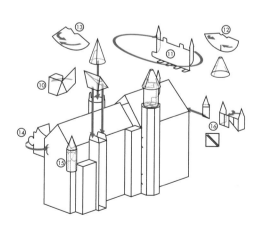

1. Take part 1, fold the sides around, and fold the roof sides to meet. Stick the roof to the tabs. Fold the end as shown and stick part 2 to the top. Fold part 3 and slot it into part 1. Fold part 4 and stick the roof to the top. Fold part 5 and slot part 4 into the side and then slot both pieces into the side of part 1.

2. Assemble part 6 in the same way as part 1. Fold the edges of part 7 and slot into the end of 6. Fold part 8 into an octagonal tube and stick. Fold the cut tabs backward and stick them to the inside of the wall on part 6 where shown. Roll part 9 into a tube and slot into part 6. Slot the tabs on the edge of part 1 into the slits in parts 8 and 9.

3. Fold and stick part 10 and stick it on top of the tower. Fold the side towers on part 11, roll to form a cylinder, and stick the towers together. Roll and stick part 12 into a cone, stick to the top of 11, and attach to the top of the tower. Do the same for 13. Roll parts 14 and 15 glue roof tab and slot the tabs into the edges of part 1. Curve the roof and stick to the tab on top. Fold parts 16 and 17 into square tubes with the turrets meeting in the middle (see square for top view). Stick on the end of 6.

MAPUNGUBWE INTERPRETATION CENTRE

Peter Rich has been researching and drawing the traditional rural settlements of South Africa since the 1970s. He works with local African building industries, applying appropriate sustainable technologies to develop new buildings. The Mapungubwe Interpretation Centre takes the form of a series of domes linked together by ramped walkways. These appear to grow out of the ground, so you cannot tell if they are ancient or modern.

FEATURES:
- *Date of construction* 2007–2009
- *Architect* Peter Rich
- *Materials* Baked earth tiles and gypsum mortar

STATUE OF LIBERTY

1. Take part 1 and fold into a box. Fold up the foot and fold the tab back underneath. Stick part 2 on the bottom of the box where shown. Rotate around and stick—this makes the bottom of the robes. Take part 3 and fold and stick the pleat as shown (see circle). Stick the pleat to the box at the top right of the base box. Roll the robe around to the back of the base box and stick.

2. Assemble the left arm (part 4) by rolling the bottom tab up inside and then folding the back inward and sticking the bottom edge to the tab. Fold the left tab inward and stick it to the inside. Flatten the top by giving it a gentle squeeze. Stick the arm to the top of the robe as shown.

3. Roll the left side of the robe around the back and then around the left arm—stick the edge to the edge of the pleat. Roll the part of the robe sticking up over the shoulder and stick it to the back.

4. Roll and stick the tab on part 5 to form the right sleeve. Stick it to the robes where shown. Take part 6, fold the edge tabs, roll them into the center, and stick them together. This will form an open cone with the flames in the middle. Roll up part 7 into a cone and stick. Stick part 6 to the hand as shown—roll the fingers around the cone. Fold up part 9 into a box and stick. Fold and stick the base (part 8). Slot the tabs into the base and stick the foot tab to the base.

5. Roll the edge of part 10 into an open cone and stick as shown. Roll the other part around and stick to the back—leave the hat sticking up. Take part 11, stick the front to the top of the face, and then roll the sides to the back of the head and stick—stick the tab first. Roll the top of the head over the back and stick. Stick the arm, head, and tablet to the body.

MASDAR INSTITUTE, ABU DHABI

FEATURES:
- *Date of construction* 2008–2010
- *Architect* Norman Foster
- *Materials* Brick, concrete, steel, glass, and ETFE

Norman Foster's Masdar Institute is the first part of a master plan for Masdar City, a new quarter of Abu Dhabi, and is powered entirely by the sun—a plentiful local resource. These six buildings, housing laboratories, teaching rooms, and apartments, respect the local style of architecture without mimicking it. So while the accommodations are shaded by traditional perforated Islamic screens, the laboratories are clad in insulating cushions of ETFE plastic.

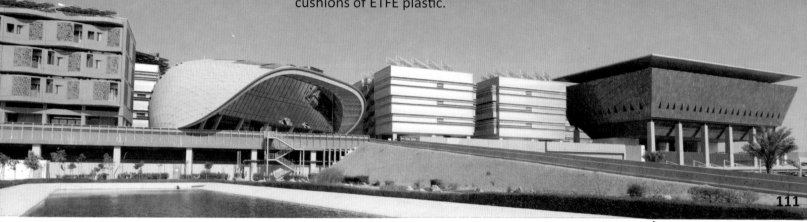

EIFFEL TOWER

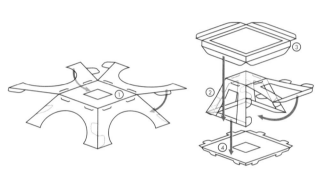

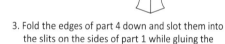

1. Take part 1 and fold the sides down. Stick the tabs to the inside of the neighboring leg.
2. Assemble the sides of part 2 in the same way and then fold the tabs at the bottom underneath. Fold the sides of part 3 down and slot the whole thing over part 2. Fold the tabs underneath. Stick this part on top of part 4.
3. Fold the edges of part 4 down and slot them into the slits on the sides of part 1 while gluing the two parts together.
4. Fold up the sides of part 5 and stick them together. Stick the base to the top of part 6. Stick part 6 to the base as shown while folding the sides down and slotting them into the slits on the side.
5. Glue parts 7, 8, 9, and 10 together to form the upper tower. Stick the tabs on the inside as shown. Fold the bottom tabs underneath and then stick to part 5. Fold the side of part 11 down and then the very bottom tabs back up inside—see the circle for a cross-section view. Stick this to the top of the tower. Slot part 12 into 13 and then into the slit in part 11.

TOWER BRIDGE

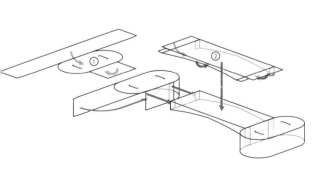

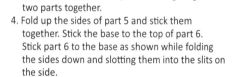

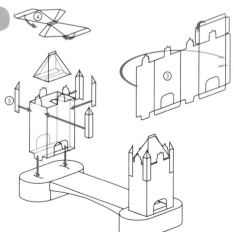

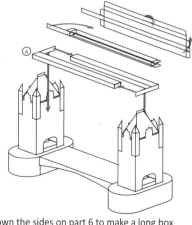

1. Take the bases (part 1) and fold the sides down. Roll the long edges around and stick the tabs on the ends to the inside of the wall. Fold down the sides of part 2, fold the tabs in, and stick the ends to the tabs. Stick the road to the bases.
2. For each tower, fold the roof and sides of part 3 to make a box. Fold the tabs on the bottom inward. Fold down the roof part 4 and stick together as shown. Fold the long tabs underneath and stick this to the top of part 3. Fold part 5 into an L shape and then fold and stick the roof to make an angle. Stick four to each corner of the tower. Attach the towers using the small tabs and slot into the base.
3. Fold down the sides on part 6 to make a long box and then glue the edge to the long tab. Fold the little tabs inward on both ends. Fold the very long tab and stick it to the little tab as shown. Do this for both parts. Stick the long tab to the end of the other part 6 and then stick it to the top of the tower, matching the artwork.

GARDENS BY THE BAY COOLED CONSERVATORIES, SINGAPORE

Singapore's Gardens by the Bay are an outstanding example of sustainability in action. Two contrasting glasshouses cover almost five acres. One features a dry Mediterranean climate in a shallow inverted bowl. The other has a cooler, moist environment in a conical structure complete with a "mountain," with a waterfall that raises humidity levels and supports the lush vertical planting—plus a helical walk that winds in and out of an exhibition about climate change.

FEATURES:

- *Date of construction* 2007–2012
- *Architects* Wilkinson Eyre, with Atelier One, Atelier Ten, and Grant Associates
- *Materials* Steel and glass

GRAND MOSQUE

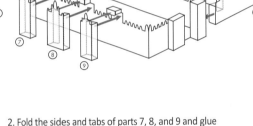

1. Take part 1 (roof) and fold down the tabs along the sides. Take part 2 (front) and make little boxes on the tops (shown in the circle). Fold the sides forward and then fold the top down. Stick the tabs together and stick to part 1. Glue walls 4 and 3 to the roof—fold the end of part 3 as shown. Fold and stick parts 5 and 6 to the side wall (4).

2. Fold the sides and tabs of parts 7, 8, and 9 and glue them to the front wall and the previously assembled boxes. Fold the end of part 10 and attach it to the wall (3). This will make a tall box. Fold and glue the outer wall (part 11) to the edge tab of wall 10 and the edge of wall 4. Fold the top and tab of part 12 and glue it to the inside of the back wall as shown.

3. Fold parts 13 and 14 and stick them to the inside of the side walls as shown, and to the tabs on part 12.

EMPIRE STATE BUILDING

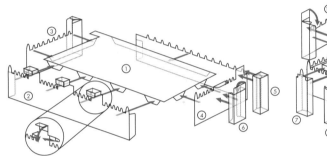

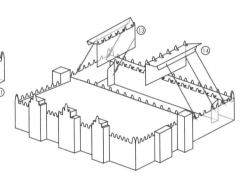

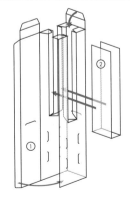

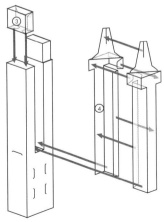

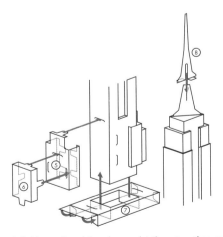

1. Take part 1 and fold to make a box shape. Glue the long tab to the long edge as shown. Fold the little tabs at the top down and then fold and stick the top to the tabs. Fold the inner tabs inward. Take part 2 and fold it as shown. Slot this in the middle of the tower and stick it to the tabs.

2. Make boxes from both part 3s and then stick them to the top of both towers as shown—line up the inner edge with the inside of the tower so they're inset from the outer edges. Fold part 4 as shown and stick them together—stick the long tabs to the opposite side and stick the very top together. Slot and stick the long piece into the center of parts 1 and 3.

3. Fold parts 5 and 6 as shown, slot them together, and then slot both into the side of the tower. Do the same on the other side. Fold the edges of the base 7 downward and stick together. Fold the inner panels down and slot onto the bottom of the tower. Fold the tabs on the end of part 8 and slot them into the slits on the top of part 4. Stick the tabs to the roof.

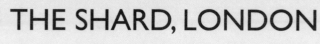

THE SHARD, LONDON

The Shard can be seen from all over London. To make the tower on such a tight site a thing of great beauty is a real achievement. It has six purposes, most taking up more than one floor: health clinic, offices, restaurants, hotel, residential apartments, and public viewing gallery—a genuine vertical village. The open top of the tower has the lightness of the Gothic spire of a German cathedral.

FEATURES:

- *Date of construction* 2009–2014
- *Architect* Renzo Piano
- *Materials* Steel and glass

CHRIST THE REDEEMER

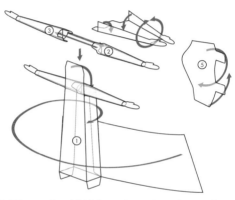

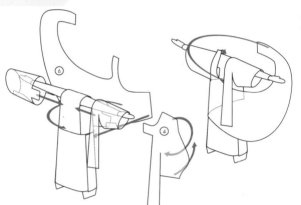

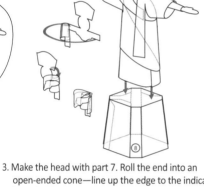

1. Take part 1 and fold the main part into a box, and stick the tab where shown. Roll up part 2 to make the left arm. Fold the two edges and roll them to meet in the middle, forming a cone in the process. Glue the middle together. Do the same with part 3, and join parts 2 and 3 together by sticking the tabs. Place on top of the body and fold the top of the body over to hold them in place. Wrap the robes around the body and stick in place.

2. Roll parts 4 and 5 into sleeves. Slide over the arms and stick the tabs to the body. Take the other part of the robes (6) and stick the edge to the back of the body where indicated. Roll the edge of the robe around to the front, going under the right arm and under the hanging piece on the left arm. Stick the right shoulder piece. Roll the end around the back, over the right shoulder, and stick the end under the hanging piece.

3. Make the head with part 7. Roll the end into an open-ended cone—line up the edge to the indicated line. This forms the neck. Roll the edge around and stick to the back of the head to form the face. Roll the top of the head back and stick it at the back and sides of the head to form the hair. Stick the bottom tab to the back of the shoulders. Assemble the base (8) and stick the statue to the top as shown.

SYDNEY HARBOUR BRIDGE

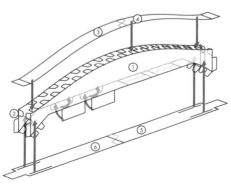

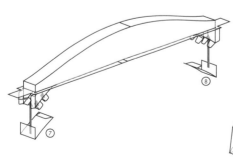

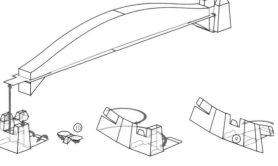

1. Fold the top tabs on both sides of the bridge (parts 1 and 2) inward. Stick parts 3 and 4 together in the middle as shown and then stick this long piece to the top and ends of the bridge. Fold up the tabs at the bottom and stick together. Stick parts 5 and 6 together. Slot the legs of the bridge through the slits in the road and stick to the tabs.

2. Fold the leg tabs inward. Fold parts 7 and 8 as shown and stick to the tabs on the legs.

3. Fold the sides of part 9 upward, fold each side inward to form two towers, and then stick the tabs. Fold the end of the base upward, fold the tab inward, and stick to the tower. Fold the edges of part 10 inward and stick them into the top of each tower. Stick the end of the bridge to the tab between the two towers. Do the same for both ends.

INDEX

GOLDEN GATE BRIDGE

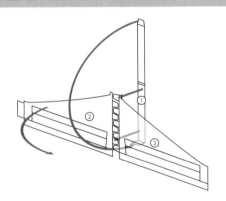
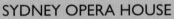
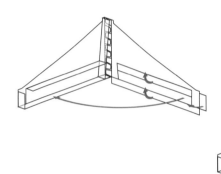

1. The four sections of the bridge are made in a similar way. There are two of every part, so use just one at a time. Take the pylon (part 1) and glue the inside edge to the tabs on the edge of parts 2 and 3 as shown. Fold the bottom of the pylon up 90 degrees and then fold the other side over the top and down. Fold the end tab in and stick it to the base. Fold the side of part 2 inward.

2. Fold up the road and the base, and fold the end in on part 2. Fold in part 3. Fold up the base and road and stick them to the same parts in part 2. Fold the end and stick it to the other end. Do the same steps for both ends.

3. Assemble the first half of the middle span with parts 4, 5, and 6 and then do the same with the other parts.

4. Attach the ends to the central spans by joining the flat sides of the pylons together. Do this for both ends.

5. Finally, join the center together by gluing the long tabs to the road.

SYDNEY OPERA HOUSE

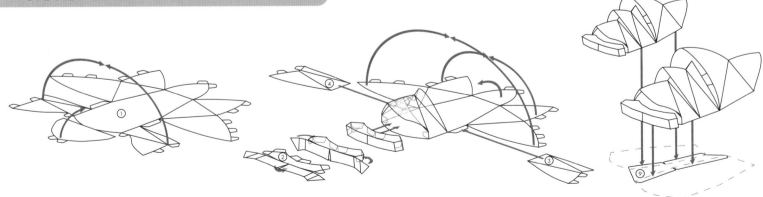

1. Take part 1 and lay it flat. Fold up the two side "petals" as shown. Fold down the tabs along the edge. Where the petals meet, slot the tabs behind its neighbor and stick together—this creates the dome. Fold up the front and stick the bottom side edges to the little tabs at the bottom, and stick the top tabs to the inside of the dome.

2. Fold part 2 as shown. Fold the sides of the front and stick to the edge tabs on the roof. Stick to the front. Attach parts 3 and 4 to the side tabs, fold up, and stick together to form the second dome. Fold the end petals up and stick together. Fold up the end and stick the tabs to the inside of the last dome.

3. Create the second, smaller building in exactly the same way as the larger one, using parts 5–8. Join the two buildings together by sticking the edges to part 9 as shown.

CN TOWER

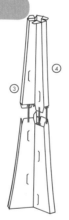

1. Make the bottom of the three-armed tower. Take one of the base parts (1) and fold it in the middle. Fold the edge tabs and stick one of the edge strips (2) to the tabs as shown. Then fold another base part and glue the tabs to the previous edge. Do this for all three pieces. The circle is a top view of how the pieces assemble.

2. Assemble the top of the tower in the same way as the bottom, using parts 3 and 4. Join the top and bottom together by slotting and gluing the tabs to the inside.

3. Slot each part 5 into the tower base where shown. Fold the top tabs of part 6 inside and glue them to the top of the tower while slotting the bottom tabs into the slits. Do this on all three sides.

4. Roll part 7 into a ring and stick. Roll parts 8 and 9 into open-ended cones. Glue the tabs on part 7 and stick to the inside of 8 and 9. Assemble 10 and 11 and stick to the bottom of 8. Roll up part 12 so the long ends meet in the middle (see circle for a cross section). Slot through and glue the tabs to part 14 as shown. Assemble and slide 13 over 12 and glue to 14. Attach 14 to 15 and then to 9. Glue this whole section the the top of the tower.

SAGRADA FAMÍLIA

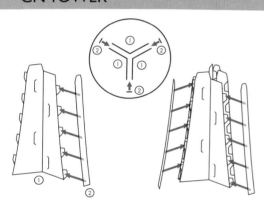

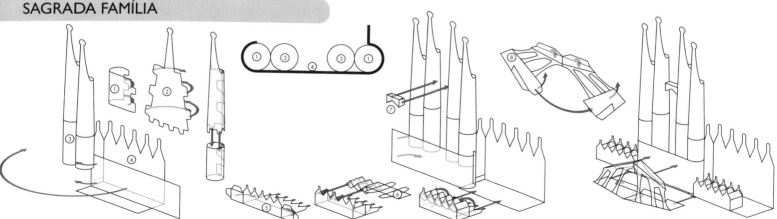

1. Make the four spires. Take part 1 and roll it into a cylinder, slot the tabs inside where they meet, and stick. Roll part 2 into a cone and stick the tabs. Stick part 2 to part 1. Do the same for all towers using part 3 for the taller ones. Fold up the back of part 4, fold the side, and stick it to the tab on the base. Fold the long side back on itself. Stick the bottom of the spires to the top of the strip—see the diagram to show how they are positioned.

2. Fold the front and the sides of part 5 as shown. Take part 6 to create the roof. Fold the roof in a zigzag as shown, and fold down the tabs on the front and back. Stick one end of the roof to the tab on the side of part 5 and then stick the roof tabs to part 5. Fold up the back and stick to the base of part 4 as shown. Do the same with the other building and glue it to the edge as shown in the next diagram. Fold part 7 and glue it between the two tall spires.

3. Take part 8 to make the front. Fold the base backward and stick the two sides together as shown. The front should now be sloping backward. Fold the tabs on the top backward and the tabs on the base upward. Stick the bottom tabs behind part 4 and the top tabs to the front.

PICTURE CREDITS

Key: t = top, b = bottom, l = left, r = right, c = center, fc = front cover

Photographs
Shutterstock: 5t Nick Pavlakis, 6 microvector, 7tc, 9t, 22r S.Borisov, 7tr Ververidis Vasilis, 8tr Sergio Bertino, 11l Iakov Kalinin, 11r Frank Bach, 12 Yury Dmitrienko / Shutterstock.com, 13 Joseph Sohm, 15l Kiev.Victor, 15r Jannis Tobias Werner, 16tl Ingrid Deelen, 17t Bule Sky Studio, 19tl DnDavis, 19tr Waj, 20tl Andrew Lam, 20tr Leslie Ray Ware, 21t andersphoto, 22tl Matt Ragen, 22l Marina99, 24l Marzolino, 24r ostill, 25t Reidl, 27l Pavel L Photo and Video / Shutterstock.com, 27r Ikunl, 28l IgorGolovniov / Shutterstock.com, 28r Morphart Creation, 28tr Dmitro2009 / Shutterstock.com, 29 lkunl, 31tl Bryant Wong, 31tc artincamera, 31tr N. F. Photography, 32l N. F. Photography, 32r S.R.Lee Photo Traveller, 33 Veronika Galkina, 35l sarra22, 35tr Aleksandra H. Kossowska, 35r JaysonPhotography, 36l Hein Nouwens, 36r Nick K, 37 wong yu liang, 39l Lena Serditova / Shutterstock.com, 39r saiko3p, 40tc Solodov Alexey / Shutterstock.com, 40r, 44l Morphart Creation, 41 fotohunter, 43l hecke61, 43r Raywoo, 43tr Hung Chung Chih, 44tl Neftali / Shutterstock.com, 45 Orhan Cam, 47c Mary Terriberry, 47r Sean Pavone / Shutterstock.com, 48tl, 48r, 52l, 56l, 64l, 64r, 68l, 80, 92 Everett Historical, 49 Ryan Rodrick Beiler, 51tl Chris Parypa Photography / Shutterstock.com, 51c Joseph Sohm / Shutterstock.com, 53 Javen, 55l, 55r, 56r Kiev.Victor, 57 Matyas Rehak, 59l mironov, 59r KPG_Payless, 60l anderm, 60c Sergey Kohl / Shutterstock.com, 60r WGXC, 61, 63r Victoria Lipov, 63l, 63c kropic1, 65 Boris Stroujko, 67tl paolo jacopo medda, 67bl gianni triggiani, 67r T.Fabian, 69 anyaivanova, 71l Ron Ellis, 71r Ttatty, 72l csp, 72r PlusONE / Shutterstock.com, 73, 75r, 76l trevor kittelty, 75tl, 76br Quick Shot / Shutterstock.com, 75bl Michele Alfieri, 76tr Boris15 / Shutterstock.com, 77 gary718, 79l pisaphotography / Shutterstock.com, 79tr Ritu Manoj Jethani / Shutterstock.com, 79br lazyllama / Shutterstock.com, 81 ndphoto / Shutterstock.com, 83l dmitry_islentev, 83tr, 83br iladm / Shutterstock.com, 84 mangostock / Shutterstock.com, 85 Taras Vyshnya, 87l Thorsten Rust, 87tr BMCL, 87br Thomas Fredriksen, 88bl ausnewsde / Shutterstock.com, 88tr Fred Kamphues, 89 Chintla, 91l FCG, 91r Ryszard Filipowicz, 93 Aleksandar Todorovic / Shutterstock.com, 95tl kuehdi / Shutterstock.com, 95bl Chris Howey / Shutterstock.com, 95r Piccia Neri / Shutterstock.com, 96l Amy Nichole Harris, 96tr Nadezda Zavitaeva / Shutterstock.com, 96br Felix Lipov / Shutterstock.com, 97 Songquan Deng, 99l Lissandra Melo / Shutterstock.com, 99r Kiev.Victor / Shutterstock.com, 100l mikecphoto / Shutterstock.com, 100r Deymos.HR / Shutterstock.com, 101 Matthew Dixon / Shutterstock.com, 103l r.nagy / Shutterstock.com, 103br catwalker / Shutterstock.com, 103tr Rachelle Burnside / Shutterstock.com, 104tl Nanisimova / Shutterstock.com, 104bl Aleks49 / Shutterstock.com, 104r Nestor Noci / Shutterstock.com, 105, 114 Frazao Production / Shutterstock.com, 106 QQ7, 107 Karol Kozlowski / Shutterstock.com, 108 David Hughes, 109 PHB.cz (Richard Semik) / Shutterstock.com, 110 MR. Interior / Shutterstock.com, 111 cristapper, 112 Frazao Production, 113 Philip Lange / Shutterstock.com, 115 Alberto Stocco / Shutterstock.com. **Wikipedia:** 16tr Public domain

Illustrations
STEFANO AZZILIN: contents t / imprint b / 3b / 4b / 5b / 6b / 7b / 8b / 9b / 10b / 11b / 12b / 13b / 14b / 19b / 20b / 21b / 22b / 23b / 24b / 25b / 26b / 27b / 28b / 29b / 30b / 31b / 32b / 33b / 34b / 35b / 36b / 37b / 38b / 39b / 40b / 41b / 42b / 47b / 48b / 49b / 50b / 51b / 52b / 53b / 54b / 55b / 56b / 57b / 58b / 59b / 60b / 61b / 62b / 63b / 64b / 65b / 66b / 71b / 72b / 73b / 74b / 75b / 76b / 77b / 78b / 79b / 80b / 81b / 82b / 87b / 88b / 89b / 90b / 91b / 92b / 93b / 94b / 95b / 96b / 97b / 98b / 103b / 104b / 105b / 106b / 107b / 108b / 109b / 110b / 111b / 112b / 113b / 114b / 115b
JANI ORBAN: 15b / 16b / 17b / 18b / 43b / 44b / 45b / 46b / 67b / 68b / 69b / 70b / 83b / 84b / 85b / 86b / 99b / 100b / 101b / 102b / 104b / 108b / 111b / 113b / 115b

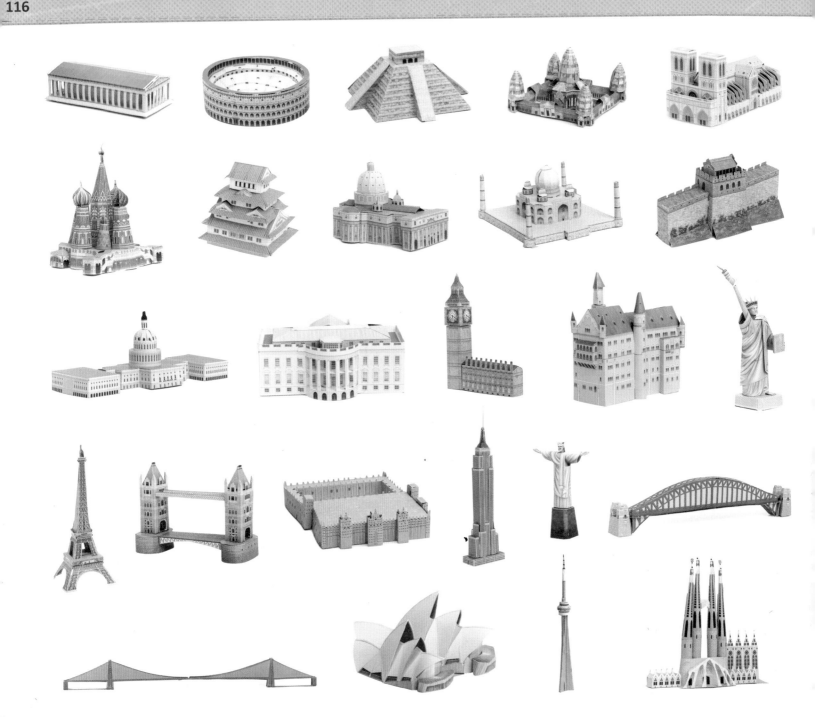